HISPANIC AMERICANS:
A Statistical Sourcebook

1999 Edition

Louise L. Hornor
Editor

information
publications

ISBN 0-929960-27-0

© 1999 Information Publications
printed in the United States of America

Printed on recycled paper.

Information Publications
3790 El Camino Real, Suite 162
Palo Alto, CA 94306
650-965-4449

HISPANIC AMERICANS:
A Statistical Sourcebook

Introduction xi

Chapter 1 - Demographics 1

Chapter 2 - Social Characteristics 21

Chapter 3 - Household & Family Characteristics 33

Chapter 4 - Education: Preprimary through High School   55

Chapter 5 - Education: Postsecondary & Educational Attainment   75

Chapter 6 - Government & Elections

Chapter 7 - The Labor Force, Employment & Unemployment

Table of Contents

Chapter 8 - Earnings, Income, Poverty, & Wealth   151

Chapter 9 - Crime & Corrections

Table of Contents

Chapter 10 - Special Topics

Introduction

Hispanic Americans: A Statistical Sourcebook is the third in a series of statistical sourcebooks covering significant topics in American life and the second in this series designed as an annual publication. This is its ninth edition. Hispanic Americans resulted from the view that, despite the fact that there is coverage of Hispanic Americans in an assortment of reference sources, there is a need for a single volume statistical reference devoted entirely to this important segment of the population.

Hispanic Americans provides an extensive collection of tables which display information on a wide variety of topics. With a few exceptions, each table presents information about the Hispanic population, the White population, and a total for Americans of all races and ethnic groups. The purpose in doing so is not to advance a specific perspective about Hispanic Americans but to provide a context within which the tabular data can be more fully understood and evaluated.

It is essential to understand before using this book that Hispanics (as viewed by most federal data collection agencies) are **not** a racial group. They are the only ethnic or cultural group on which the federal government gathers data. Persons of Hispanic origin may be Hispanic and white, or Hispanic and black, or Hispanic and Asian, etc. As a general guideline, the overwhelming majority of persons who identify themselves as Hispanic also identify themselves as white for federal data collection purposes.

Presenting data by race and ethnicity always puts one at risk of being labeled racist. Although undoubtedly there will be persons on both sides - those who see Hispanic Americans as a propagandistic derogation of the Hispanic community and those who feel that the book eloquently proves the inherent prejudice of our culture - the intent here is to serve neither cause. In fact, Hispanic Americans is not intended to serve any cause or advance any point of view but to serve as a reportorial resource, providing access to federal government information. By researching and presenting this sometimes difficult to find, hard to understand information, Hispanic Americans can serve students, business persons, social scientists, researchers, and others who need basic data about Hispanic Americans.

The use of the term 'Hispanic' itself can also be a cause for controversy. A number of terms have been used by Hispanic Americans to name themselves, such as Latino and Spanish. Hispanic is used here solely because it is the word currently used by the federal government in gathering data. In some surveys, data is further analyzed into subgroups of the Hispanic population (e.g., Mexican Americans, Cuban-Americans, etc.). Where such data is available in this detail, it is presented here.

Another sensitive question is, who is Hispanic? For federal data collection purposes, Hispanic persons are those who say they are Hispanic (or, Spanish, Latino, etc.). For statistical reporting purposes, being Hispanic is based solely on the self-identification of the respondent.

As was stated, most agencies of the federal government consider Hispanic to be a supplement to racial categories. However, some agencies collect data as if Hispanic origin was a racial category. For example, the Centers for Disease Control collects data about AIDS using the classifications of White non-Hispanic, Black non-Hispanic, and Hispanic. The Department of Education also collects data in this manner. These agencies are the exception to the rule, and such exceptions are noted in the table notes at the end of each table.

Organization

The main portion of this book has been divided into ten chapters of tables:

Chapter 1:   Demographics
Chapter 2:   Social Characteristics
Chapter 3:   Household & Family Characteristics
Chapter 4:   Education: Preprimary through High School
Chapter 5:   Education: Postsecondary & Educational Attainment
Chapter 6:   Government & Elections
Chapter 7:   The Labor Force, Employment & Unemployment
Chapter 8:   Earnings, Income, Poverty, & Wealth
Chapter 9:   Crime & Corrections
Chapter 10:   Special Topics

The tables in each chapter represent results of a comprehensive review of all available federal government statistical information on the Hispanic population. This material was edited and organized into chapters and arranged in a sequence roughly following the pattern found in publications of the U.S. Bureau of the Census.

Each table presents pertinent information from the source or sources in a clear, comprehensible fashion. As users of this book will likely be a diverse group ranging from librarians to business planners, from social scientists to marketers, all with different uses for the same data, the information selected for presentation was chosen for its broad scope and general appeal.

The Sources

All of the information in <u>Hispanic Americans</u> comes from U.S. Government sources either originally or by way of republication by the federal government. In turn, most of the federal information is from the U.S. Bureau of the Census. Without question, the Bureau is the largest data gathering organization in the nation. It collects information on an exceptionally broad range of topics, not only for its own use and for the use of Congress and the Executive, but also for other federal agencies and departments. The reach of the Bureau is wider than most people realize. It encompasses the decennial Census of Population, the Current Population Survey, and the Annual Housing Survey. In cooperation with other agencies, the Bureau extends to the Consumer Expenditure Survey, the National Crime Survey, the National Family Growth Survey, and many others. The fact that the Bureau is responsible for so much of the federal government's data collection adds uniformity to the statistical information published by different agencies. Although the uniformity is not complete, there is enough to make the work of data users a lot easier. The influence of the Bureau of the Census extends beyond federal government data collection. Because of the sheer volume of data it collects, many private data collectors have adopted some of its procedures and terminology. This has the added value for researchers of making private and public data more compatible.

Observant readers will note that the source of many tables is a Census publication, <u>Statistical Abstract of the United States</u>. There are a number of reasons for this. First, due to federal budget cuts, a growing quantity of information used in <u>Statistical Abstract</u> has never been published elsewhere before or it has never been published in such a detailed way. Second, as the preeminent federal data publisher, the Census Bureau has access to a wealth of raw data in machine readable form. It is able to aggregate data geographically on regional lines and break out other detail such as age, sex, race, etc., using its own parameters for publication. Thus, even when information is published elsewhere, the manner of presentation in <u>Statistical Abstract</u> is likely to be unique. Data from this source is presented in a more general way so as to be useful to many different types of data users.

On all tables where <u>Statistical Abstract</u> is cited as the source, the original source also has been checked for additional information. To make more detailed research easier, <u>Statistical Abstract's</u> own source (if it is not the Bureau itself), is listed as well.

Types of Information

Regardless of its source, there are basically two types of data presented in the tables of this book.

The first is complete count data. For example, the five questions asked of all Americans by the Bureau of the Census in its decennial census was an attempt at a complete count of a given universe.

The second type of data is survey information. Here a fairly large, specifically chosen segment of a population is studied. This sample is drawn to be statistically representative of the entire population or universe. Information about housing units and money income are some of the items in this book based on this type of survey information. Of course, survey information is only as good as the survey itself; therefore, the reader should always be the judge of the significance and accuracy of the material presented as it applies to his or her own research. Although specific survey methodology is not discussed here, a full reference to each source is made on every table. Interested readers may consult the original source materials, which in most cases contain a detailed explanation of survey methodology.

The Tables

This section details how the tables have been prepared and presented. Table titles are the first source of valuable information:

Table 4.01   School Enrollment, by Age, 1985, 1991, 1996

The table number contains the chapter number to the left of the decimal and the location of the table within the chapter to the right of the decimal. Thus Table 4.01 is the first table of Chapter 4. With a few exceptions, tables have been arranged within a chapter to present the oldest, most general information first, followed by newer, more specific information. This pattern is mirrored in the tables themselves, which present the oldest, most general information at the beginning.

In a table title, the word or words before the first comma identify the general topic of the table. Following the first comma is descriptive wording which identifies the detail presented about the general topic; i.e., the data is presented by age, sex, marital status, etc., in this case, by age. After the description of the presentation of the data, the years for which data is presented are shown.

It should be noted that both the table titles and the tables themselves retain the original terms of the source material. This has the advantage of making the book compatible with the original sources.

To further facilitate use, every table in the book presents data in two, three, five, or six columns. The left-most column or columns are for the Hispanic population; the center column or columns are for the White population; and the right-hand column or columns present data for all races and/or ethnic groups. For data which is available in subgroups of the Hispanic population, a separate six column table is provided, with columns for Hispanics of Mexican origin, Puerto Rican origin, Cuban origin, Central/South American origin, other Hispanic origin, and a total of all persons of Hispanic origin.

Along the left margin of each table appears a column of line descriptors. Here, after a general heading, subgroups of the heading (usually indented) are shown. Two principles cover arranging and presenting the line descriptors: the oldest, most general information appears first, progressing to the newer, more specific; and quantities appear first, followed by percentages, medians, means, and per capita amounts.

Wherever available and appropriate, a time span of data is presented, usually going back five to ten years. This provides readers with a historical context for the information. However, readers should be cautioned that the years selected have been chosen from no special knowledge of the subject, nor to make any specific point. Thus the fact that there has been a decrease or increase in a given indicator for the period displayed does not mean that the same trend will continue, or that it represents the continuation of a historical trend, or even that which appears to be a trend within this period actually is one. The time span and specific dates have been chosen largely to create a congruity of data, and a basis of comparison between different categories of information.

Table Notes

At the bottom of each table three key paragraphs appear: Source, Notes, and Units. The **Source** paragraph lists the source of the data presented in the table. When more than one source was used, the sources are listed in the same order in which the data itself appears in the table. As all sources are government publications, the issuing agency is listed as the author. All citations provide both the page and table number in the source from which the material was taken. This bibliographic detail on each table makes a separate bibliography at the end of the book unnecessary. A Superintendent of Documents Classification Number is also provided. This number is used as a locator number in most government depository libraries, and documents are shelved or filed according to it, just the way books in some public libraries are organized by the Dewey Decimal System.

In some cases, the data has been downloaded from government sites on the World Wide Web. In this case, the Universal Resource Locator (URL) is given.

The paragraph of **Notes** includes pertinent facts about the data, the time of year covered by the survey, and the scope of the survey universe. In those case where Hispanic origin is a separate race-like category (i.e., where the data is collected in such a way that one can be either Hispanic or white, but not both), this is stated. One general note can be made here at the outset about all tabular data: detail (subgroups) may not add to the total shown, due to either rounding or the fact that only selected subgroups are displayed.

The final paragraph of a table, **Units,** identifies the units used, specifically stating that the quantity is millions of persons, thousands of workers, dollars per capita, etc. Readers are urged to pay special attention to this especially when a median, mean, percent, rate, or a per capita amount is provided.

The Index

Every key term from the tables has been indexed. Readers should note that the index provides table numbers as opposed to page numbers.

The Glossary

It is important to be clear about terminology in a work such as this. Not only does the government have overtly specialized terms which clearly require a definition or explanation, but many government agencies use ordinary words in specialized ways. There are real differences between: a household and a family; a family and a married couple; the resident population and the civilian non-institutional population; a service industry and a service occupation; an urban area and a metropolitan area; to name just a few. All specialized terms are defined either in the table or in the glossary. Needless to say, it is absolutely vital to understand the meaning of all terms used in a table before drawing any conclusions from the data. When in doubt, consult the glossary.

For many tables, it is not possible to fully define a term or concept in the table notes, so the glossary serves as an important tool in using the tables. All terms that appear in either the title or text of a table which may be unclear or are used in a special way are defined in the glossary. Wherever possible, the definition is adapted (and in many cases taken verbatim) from the definition provided in the source publication. Not all source materials provide definitions, so sometimes a definition has been constructed by reviewing and summarizing explanatory and supplementary material from the source.

In compiling the glossary the intention was to provide short clear definitions, including only as much background material as necessary to make a term understandable. However, in practice this resulted in compromises. For certain terms (such as metropolitan area concepts), some methodological background is essential in order to achieve an understanding. Where such background is vital it has been included. Readers requiring additional technical or methodological detail are referred to the sources for more complete explanations.

A Suggestion on How to Use This Book

One way to use this book is by locating the subject of general interest in the Table of Contents, and turning to that chapter. While the Table of Contents is detailed enough to narrow a search and the index can speed access to specific items, sometimes paging through the dozen or so tables in a given field uncovers unanticipated information of genuine importance. It is just this type of serendipity that has lead to the inclusion of information in this book, and sometimes such an unexpected find can greatly enhance a research project.

A Final Word

As this book is updated on an annual basis, questions, comments, and criticisms from users are vital to making informed editorial choices about succeeding editions. If you have a suggestion or comment, be assured that it will be both appreciated and carefully considered. If you should find an error here, please let us know so that it may be corrected. Our goal is to provide accurate, easy to use, statistical compendiums which serve our readers' needs. Your help enables us to do our job better.

Chapter 1: Demographics

Table 1.01   Resident Population and Median Age, 1980 - 1997

| | Hispanic | | White | | Total | |
	total	median age	total	median age	total	median age
1980 (April 1)	14,609	23.2	194,713	30.9	226,546	30.0
1985 (July 1)	17,865	na	202,769	32.4	235,736	31.4
1986 (July 1)	18,523	na	204,326	32.7	241,096	31.7
1987 (July 1)	19,183	25.1	205,833	33.0	243,400	32.1
1988 (July 1)	19,847	25.8	207,357	33.1	245,807	32.3
1989 (July 1)	20,505	26.1	208,961	33.6	248,240	32.7
1990 (April 1)	22,354	na	199,686	na	248,710	32.8
1991 (July 1)	23,350	25.7	210,899	34.1	252,177	33.1
1992 (July 1)	24,238	25.8	212,912	34.4	255,082	33.4
1994 (July 1)	26,077	26.1	216,470	35.0	260,341	34.0
1995 (July 1)	26,994	26.2	218,085	35.3	262,755	34.3
1996 (July 1)	28,269	26.4	219,749	35.7	265,284	34.6
1997 (July 1)	29,348	26.4	221,334	36.0	267,636	34.9

SOURCE: U.S. Bureau of the Census, Statistical Abstract of the United States, 1989, p. 17, table 21; 1990, p. 17, table 19; 1991, p. 17, table 19; 1993, p. 14, table 12, p. 15, table 14, page 23, table 24; 1994, pp. 22-23, table 22; 1995, pp. 22-23, table 22; 1996, pp. 22-23, table 22; 1997, pp. 22-23, table 22, 1998, pp. 22-23, table 22. C 3.134:(year)

NOTES: 'Total' includes other races and ethnic groups not shown separately.

UNITS: Population in thousands of persons; median age in years.

Table 1.02 Resident Population, by Age and Sex, 1980, 1985, 1997

	Hispanic	White	Total
1980			
Both sexes			
total	14,609	194,713	226,546
under 5 years old	1,663	13,414	16,348
16 years old and older	8,328	149,121	171,196
65 years old and older	709	23,162	25,549
male			
total	2,280	94,924	110,053
under 5 years old	848	6,882	8,362
16 years old and older	4,075	71,559	81,766
65 years old and older	305	9,316	10,305
female			
total	7,329	99,788	116,493
under 5 years old	815	6,532	7,986
16 years old and older	4,252	77,562	89,429
65 years old and older	404	13,846	15,245
1985			
Both sexes			
total	16,940	202,768	238,740
under 5 years old	1,809	14,636	18,037
16 years old and older	10,222	157,584	183,010
65 years old and older	819	25,743	28,530
male			
total	8,441	99,006	116,161
under 5 years old	923	7,509	9,230
16 years old and older	5,019	75,820	87,631
65 years old and older	353	10,390	11,529
female			
total	8,499	103,762	122,579
under 5 years old	886	7,127	8,806
16 years old and older	5,202	81,764	95,379
65 years old and older	466	15,353	17,002

continued on the next page

Table 1.02   continued

	Hispanic	White	Total
1997			
Both sexes			
total	29,348	221,334	267,636
under 5 years old	3,347	15,184	19,150
5-13 years old	4,941	27,620	34,949
14-17 years old	2,040	12,231	15,429
85 years old and older	160	3,504	3,871
male			
total	15,074	108,893	131,018
under 5 years old	1,717	7,789	9,801
5-13 years old	2,529	14,168	17,896
14-17 years old	1,067	6,318	7,950
85 years old and older	54	998	1,112
female			
total	14,274	112,441	136,618
under 5 years old	1,630	7,396	9,349
5-13 years old	2,413	13,453	17,053
14-17 years old	975	5,913	7,479
85 years old and older	106	2,507	2,759

SOURCE: U.S. Bureau of the Census, Statistical Abstract of the United States, 1985, p. 28, table 30; 1987, p. 18, table 20; 1996, p. 21, table 21, p. 24, table 23; 1998, p. 21, table 21, p. 24, table 23 (data from U.S-. Bureau of the Census, *Current Population Reports*, Series P-25). C 3.134:(year)

NOTES: 'All races' includes other races and ethnic groups not shown separately.

UNITS: Resident population in thousands of persons.

Table 1.03 Hispanic Population, by Type of Origin, by Age, 1997

				type of origin		
	Mexican	Puerto Rican	Cuban	Central/ South Amer	other Hispanic	total Hispanic
1997						
Total population	100.0%	100.0%	100.0%	100.0%	100.0%	100.0%
0-4 years old	12.8	9.9	6.1	9.6	10.3	11.6
5-9 years old	11.0	9.7	5.5	7.9	9.4	10.1
10-14 years old	9.1	10.6	4.6	6.8	7.8	8.6
15-19 years old	8.9	10.7	3.4	9.3	8.1	8.9
20-24 years old	9.4	6.1	5.2	8.8	8.5	8.7
25-29 years old	9.9	7.3	5.5	10.2	8.3	9.4
30-34 years old	8.9	8.9	10.4	10.4	8.8	9.1
35-39 years old	7.8	8.4	8.2	10.1	8.8	8.3
40-44 years old	6.1	7.3	7.7	7.0	7.5	6.5
45-49 years old	4.2	5.0	5.9	5.6	4.3	4.6
50-54 years old	3.5	4.0	3.4	4.2	4.3	3.7
55-59 years old	2.5	4.4	6.3	3.9	3.9	3.2
60-64 years old	1.9	2.4	7.2	2.1	3.0	2.3
65-69 years old	1.5	1.8	7.2	1.6	2.7	1.9
70-74 years old	1.2	1.5	5.8	1.3	1.4	1.5
75-79 years old	0.7	0.9	3.3	0.7	1.5	0.9
80-84 years old	0.4	0.5	2.1	0.3	0.5	0.5
85 and older	0.3	0.6	2.3	0.3	0.9	0.4

SOURCE: U.S. Census Bureau, "Hispanic Population of the United States, (Table 1.2). March, 1997 CPS: Age by Race-Ethnicity: Both Sexes - Percents"; released 7 August 1998; <http://www.census.gov/population/socdemo/hispanic/cps97/tab01-2.txt>

NOTES: Total population includes other races and ethnic groups not shown separately. 'Other Hispanic origin' includes persons from Spain and persons identifying themselves generally as Hispanic, Spanish, Spanish-American, Hispano, Latino, etc.

UNITS: Percent as a percent of total shown (100.0%).

Table 1.04 Hispanic Population, by Type of Origin, by Sex, 1985, 1990, 1997

	male	female	both sexes
1985			
Total resident population	48.5%	51.5%	100.0%
total Hispanic population	49.8	50.2	100.0
by origin			
Mexican origin	51.1%	48.9%	100.0%
Puerto Rican origin	46.8	53.2	"
Cuban origin	48.7	51.3	"
Central/South American origin	47.9	52.1	"
other Hispanic origin	49.1	50.9	"
not of Hispanic origin	48.4	51.6	100.0
1990			
Total resident population	48.7%	51.3%	100.0%
total Hispanic population	50.2·	49.8	100.0
by origin			
Mexican origin	51.2%	48.8%	100.0%
Puerto Rican origin	47.9	52.1	"
Cuban origin	48.4	51.6	"
Central/South American origin	48.8	51.2	"
other Hispanic origin	48.1	51.9	"
not of Hispanic origin	48.5%	51.5%	100.0%
1997			
Total resident population	49.0%	51.0%	100.0%
total Hispanic population	51.3	48.7	100.0
by origin			
Mexican origin	52.2	47.8	100.0
Puerto Rican origin	47.6	52.4	"
Cuban origin	53.5	46.5	"
Central/South American origin	50.5	49.5	"
other Hispanic origin	49.4	50.6	"
not of Hispanic origin	48.7	51.3	100.0

SOURCE: U.S. Bureau of the Census, The Hispanic Population in the United States: March, 1985, p. 12, table 1 (data from U.S. Bureau of the Census, *Current Population Reports*). C 3.186:P-20/422

U.S. Bureau of the Census, The Hispanic Population in the United States: March, 1990, pp. 86-7 table 1; (data from U.S. Bureau of the Census, *Current Population Reports*). C 3.186/14-2:990

U.S. Census Bureau, "Hispanic Population of the United States, (Table 1.5). March, 1997 CPS: Age of Race-Ethnicity: Both Sexes - Total Percents;" released 7 August 1998; <http://www.census.gov/population/socdemo/hispanic/cps97/tab01-5.txt>.

NOTES: 'Other Hispanic origin' includes persons from Spain and persons identifying themselves generally as Hispanic, Spanish, Spanish-American, Hispano, Latino, etc.

UNITS: Resident population in percent, by sex, as a percent of all persons.

Table 1.05   Population Projections, by Age and Sex, 2000 - 2025

	Hispanic	White	Total
2000			
all ages	31,366	225,532	274,634
under 5 years old	3,203	14,724	18,987
5-13 years old	5,651	28,254	36,043
14-17 years old	2,179	12,412	15,752
18-24 years old	3,679	20,852	26,258
25-34 years old	5,181	29,837	37,233
35-44 years old	4,836	36,762	44,659
45-54 years old	3,049	31,247	37,030
55-64 years old	1,717	20,600	23,962
65-74 years old	1,120	15,846	18,136
75-84 years old	568	11,131	12,315
85 years old and over	183	3,866	4,259
Male	15,799	110,799	134,181
Female	15,566	114,734	140,453
2005			
all ages	36,057	232,463	285,981
under 5 years old	3,580	14,618	19,127
5-13 years old	6,215	27,716	35,850
14-17 years old	2,672	13,177	16,986
18-24 years old	4,270	22,306	28,268
25-34 years old	5,414	28,705	36,306
35-44 years old	5,421	34,201	42,165
45-54 years old	3,927	34,574	41,507
55-64 years old	2,260	25,334	29,606
65-74 years old	1,308	15,844	18,369
75-84 years old	748	11,553	12,898
85 years old and over	242	4,434	4,899
Male	18,082	114,350	139,785
Female	17,975	118,113	146,196

continued on the next page

Table 1.05   continued

	Hispanic	White	Total
2010			
all ages	41,139	239,588	297,716
under 5 years old	4,080	15,142	20,012
5-13 years old	6,654	27,087	35,605
14-17 years old	3,007	12,951	16,894
18-24 years old	5,101	23,489	30,138
25-34 years old	6,059	30,099	38,292
35-44 years old	5,562	30,646	38,521
45-54 years old	4,833	35,911	43,564
55-64 years old	2,997	29,845	35,283
65-74 years old	1,606	18,101	21,057
75-84 years old	896	11,208	12,680
85 years old and over	345	5,108	5,671
Male	20,557	118,000	145,584
Female	20,582	121,588	152,132
2025			
all ages	58,930	262,227	335,050
under 5 years old	5,662	16,630	22,498
5-13 years old	9,479	29,949	40,413
14-17 years old	3,944	13,166	17,872
18-24 years old	6,560	22,702	30,372
25-34 years old	8,748	32,831	43,119
35-44 years old	7,345	32,869	42,391
45-54 years old	5,791	29,010	36,890
55-64 years old	5,272	32,246	39,542
65-74 years old	3,595	29,733	35,425
75-84 years old	1,771	16,969	19,481
85 years old and over	763	6,122	7,046
Male	29,276	129,596	164,119
Female	29,654	132,631	170,931

SOURCE: U.S. Bureau of the Census, Statistical Abstract of the United States, 1996, p. 25, table 24; p. 26, table 25; (data from U.S. Bureau of the Census, *Current Population Reports*, Series P-25). C 3.134:996

NOTES: 'Total' includes other races and ethnic groups not shown separately. Population projections as of July 1, of the year shown.

UNITS: Estimates of the total population in thousands of persons, includes armed forces overseas. Based on Series 14 - Middle Series.

Table 1.06   Population Projections, by Sex, 2000 - 2025

	Hispanic	White	Total
2000			
both sexes	31,366	225,532	274,634
male	15,799	110,799	134,181
female	15,566	114,734	140,453
2005			
both sexes	36,057	232,463	285,981
male	18,082	114,350	139,785
female	17,975	118,113	146,196
2010			
both sexes	41,139	239,588	297,716
male	20,557	118,000	145,584
female	20,582	121,588	152,132
2025			
both sexes	58,930	262,227	335,050
male	29,276	129,596	164,119
female	29,654	132,631	170,931

SOURCE: U.S. Bureau of the Census, Statistical Abstract of the United States, 1996, p. 25, table 24; p. 26, table 25; (data from U.S. Bureau of the Census, *Current Population Reports*, Series P-25). C 3.134:996

NOTES: 'Total' includes other races and ethnic groups not shown separately. Population projections as of July 1, of the year shown.

UNITS: Estimates of the total population in thousands of persons, includes armed forces overseas. Based on Series 14 - Middle Series.

Table 1.07   Population Projections, 1995 - 2050 (revised)

	Hispanic	White	Total
1995	26,936	218,078	262,820
1996	27,804	219,641	265,253
1997	28,680	221,163	267,645
1998	29,566	222,648	270,002
1999	30,461	224,103	272,330
2000	31,366	225,532	274,634
2005	36,057	232,463	285,981
2010	41,139	239,588	297,716
2015	46,705	247,193	310,134
2020	52,652	254,887	322,742
2025	58,930	262,227	335,050
2030	65,570	269,046	346,899
2035	72,639	275,470	358,457
2040	80,164	281,720	369,980
2045	88,125	288,016	381,713
2050	96,508	294,615	393,931

SOURCE: U.S. Bureau of the Census, <u>Current Population Reports: Population Projections of the United States By Age, Sex, Race, and Hispanic Origin, 1995 - 2050</u>, Series P-25, #1130, pp. 32-37, table 1. C 3.186: P-25/1104

NOTES: 'Total' includes other races and ethnic groups not shown separately. Population projections as of July 1, of the year shown.

UNITS: Estimates of the total population in thousands of persons, includes armed forces overseas. Based on Series 14 - Middle Series.

Table 1.08   Resident Population, by State, 1980

	Hispanic	White	Total
Alabama	34	2,873	3,894
Alaska	9	310	402
Arizona	444	2,241	2,718
Arkansas	17	1,890	2,286
California	4,541	18,031	23,668
Colorado	341	2,571	2,890
Connecticut	125	2,799	3,108
Delaware	10	488	594
District of Columbia	18	172	638
Florida	585	8,185	9,746
Georgia	61	3,947	5,463
Hawaii	71	319	965
Idaho	37	902	944
Illinois	635	9,233	11,427
Indiana	87	5,004	5,490
Iowa	26	2,839	2,914
Kansas	63	2,168	2,364
Kentucky	27	3,379	3,661
Louisiana	100	2,912	4,206
Maine	5	1,110	1,125
Maryland	63	3,159	4,217
Massachusetts	141	5,363	5,737
Michigan	158	7,872	9,262
Minnesota	32	3,936	4,076
Mississippi	24	1,615	2,521
Missouri	52	4,345	4,917
Montana	10	740	787
Nebraska	28	1,490	1,570
Nevada	54	700	800
New Hampshire	5	910	921
New Jersey	494	6,127	7,365
New Mexico	477	978	1,303
New York	1,661	13,961	17,558

continued on the next page

Table 1.08   continued

	Hispanic	White	Total
North Carolina	56	4,458	5,882
North Dakota	3	626	653
Ohio	120	9,597	10,798
Oklahoma	58	2,598	3,025
Oregon	66	2,491	2,633
Pennsylvania	154	10,652	11,864
Rhode Island	19	897	947
South Carolina	34	2,147	3,122
South Dakota	4	640	691
Tennessee	34	3,835	4,591
Texas	2,983	11,198	14,229
Utah	60	1,383	1,461
Vermont	3	507	511
Virginia	80	4,230	5,347
Washington	121	3,779	4,132
West Virginia	13	1,875	1,950
Wisconsin	63	4,443	4,706
Wyoming	25	446	470

SOURCE: U.S. Bureau of the Census, Census of Population: General Population Characteristics: United States Summary PC80-1-B1, p. 1-125, table 62.   C 3.223/6:980/B1
U.S. Bureau of the Census, Census of Population: General Social and Economic Characteristics: United States Summary PC80-1-C1, p. 1-280, table 233.   C 3.223/7:980/C1

NOTES: 'Total' includes other races and ethnic groups not shown separately.

UNITS: Population in thousands of persons.

Table 1.09   Resident Population, by State, 1990

	Hispanic	White	Total
Alabama	25	2,976	4,041
Alaska	18	415	550
Arizona	688	2,963	3,665
Arkansas	20	1,945	2,351
California	7,688	20,524	29,760
Colorado	424	2,905	3,294
Connecticut	213	2,859	3,287
Delaware	16	535	666
District of Columbia	33	180	607
Florida	1,574	10,749	12,938
Georgia	109	4,600	6,478
Hawaii	81	370	1,108
Idaho	53	950	1,007
Illinois	904	8,953	11,431
Indiana	99	5,021	5,544
Iowa	33	2,683	2,777
Kansas	94	2,232	2,478
Kentucky	22	3,392	3,685
Louisiana	93	2,839	4,220
Maine	7	1,208	1,228
Maryland	125	3,394	4,781
Massachusetts	288	5,405	6,016
Michigan	202	7,756	9,295
Minnesota	54	4,130	4,375
Mississippi	16	1,633	2,573
Missouri	62	4,486	5,117
Montana	12	741	799
Nebraska	37	1,481	1,578
Nevada	124	1,013	1,202
New Hampshire	11	1,087	1,109
New Jersey	740	6,130	7,730
New Mexico	579	1,146	1,515

continued on the next page

Table 1.09   continued

	Hispanic	White	Total
New York	2,214	13,385	17,990
North Carolina	77	5,008	6,629
North Dakota	5	604	639
Ohio	140	9,522	10,847
Oklahoma	86	2,584	3,146
Oregon	113	2,637	2,842
Pennsylvania	232	10,520	11,882
Rhode Island	46	917	1,003
South Carolina	31	2,407	3,487
South Dakota	5	638	696
Tennessee	33	4,048	4,877
Texas	4,340	12,775	16,987
Utah	85	1,616	1,723
Vermont	4	555	563
Virginia	160	4,792	6,187
Washington	215	4,309	4,867
West Virginia	8	1,792	1,856
Wisconsin	93	4,513	4,892
Wyoming	26	427	454

SOURCE: U.S. Bureau of the Census, Statistical Abstract of the United States, 1991, p. 22, table 27 (data from U.S. Bureau of the Census, *Press Release CB91-100*. C 3.134:991

NOTES: 'Total' includes other races and ethnic groups not shown separately.

UNITS: Population in thousands of persons.

Table 1.10   Hispanic Population, Selected Metropolitan Areas, 1996

	Hispanic population	percent of total
Los Angeles-Riverside-Orange County, CA CMSA	5,850	37.8%
New York-Northern New Jersey-Long Island, NY-NJ-CT-PA CMSA/NECMA	3,325	16.8
Miami-Fort Lauderdale, FL CMSA	1,286	36.6
San Francisco-Oakland-San Jose, CA CMSA	1,228	18.6
Chicago-Gary-Kenosha, IL-IN-WI CMSA	1,125	13.1
Houston-Galveston-Brazoria, TX CMSA	1,005	23.6
San Antonio, TX MSA	777	52.1
Dallas-Fort Worth, TX CMSA	690	15.1
San Diego, CA MSA	666	25.1
Phoenix-Mesa, AZ MSA	536	19.5
El Paso, TX MSA	503	73.5
McAllen-Edinburg-Mission, TX MSA	433	87.3
Fresno, CA MSA	355	41.2
Washington-Baltimore, DC-MD-VA-WV CMSA	351	4.9
Denver-Boulder-Greeley, CO CMSA	320	14.0
Boston-Worcester-Lawrence-Lowell Brockton, MA-NH-NECMA	297	5.1
Philadelphia-Wilmington-Atlantic City, PA-NJ-DE-MD CMSA	278	4.7
Brownsville-Harlingen-San Benito, TX MSA	266	84.4
Albuquerque, NM MSA	257	38.4
Austin-San Marcos, TX MSA	253	24.3
Sacramento-Yolo, CA CMSA	235	14.4
Corpus Christi, TX MSA	217	56.5
Tucson, AZ MSA	214	27.9
Bakersfield, CA MSA	211	33.8

Table 1.10   continued

	Hispanic population	percent of total
Tampa-St. Petersburg-Clearwater, FL MSA	189	8.6
Las Vegas, NV-AZ MSA	169	14.1
Laredo, TX MSA	168	94.9
Visalia-Tulare-Porterville, CA MSA	157	44.9
Orlando, FL MSA	149	10.5
Stockton-Lodi, CA MSA	148	27.7
Salinas, CA MSA	135	39.9
Seattle-Tacoma-Bremerton, WA CMSA	133	4.0
Detroit-Ann Arbor-Flint, MI CMSA	124	2.3
Santa Barbara-Santa Maria-Lompoc, CA MSA	124	32.1
Portland-Salem, OR-WA CMSA	115	5.6
Modesto, CA MSA	111	26.7
Atlanta, GA MSA	105	3.0

SOURCE: U.S. Bureau of the Census, Statistical Abstract of the United States, 1998, p. 45, table 45. C 3.134:998

NOTES: Metropolitan Areas are shown in rank order of Hispanic population of CMSA's and MSA's. Areas as defined by US Office of Management and Budget, December 31, 1992.

UNITS: Population in thousands of persons; percent as a percent of the total metropolitan area population.

Table 1.11 Resident Population, by State, Projections for 2020

	Hispanic	White	Total
Alabama	1.2%	72.0%	5,231
Alaska	4.8	65.2	866
Arizona	31.7	85.0	5,713
Arkansas	1.9	83.1	3,005
California	36.5	71.0	47,953
Colorado	20.0	90.1	4,871
Connecticut	12.9	85.2	3,617
Delaware	5.9	70.7	871
District of Columbia	6.1	33.0	636
Florida	21.5	78.9	19,449
Georgia	3.2	66.9	9,426
Hawaii	13.7	47.9	1,815
Idaho	11.7	95.3	1,600
Illinois	15.7	75.2	13,218
Indiana	4.0	87.7	6,488
Iowa	3.2	94.6	3,038
Kansas	7.9	87.4	3,130
Kentucky	1.0	89.7	4,313
Louisiana	3.6	63.9	5,193
Maine	1.4	97.7	1,400
Maryland	5.0	59.6	6,289
Massachusetts	9.9	86.5	6,363
Michigan	4.6	77.0	10,377
Minnesota	2.8	90.1	5,426
Mississippi	1.0	63.1	3,100
Missouri	2.2	85.5	6,123
Montana	2.6	90.4	1,071
Nebraska	6.5	92.5	1,885
Nevada	26.1	81.3	2,145
New Hampshire	2.2	95.6	1,399
New Jersey	17.0	73.5	9,058
New Mexico	55.4	82.7	2,338

continued on the next page

Table 1.11   continued

	Hispanic	White	Total
New York	15.9%	70.6%	19,111
North Carolina	2.4	72.3	9,014
North Dakota	1.4	90.8	719
Ohio	2.9	83.8	11,870
Oklahoma	5.0	80.0	4,020
Oregon	8.1	89.1	4,367
Pennsylvania	4.9	85.4	12,656
Rhode Island	11.3	88.6	1,090
South Carolina	1.8	66.5	4,685
South Dakota	1.6	83.7	863
Tennessee	1.3	80.6	6,434
Texas	40.3	82.9	25,592
Utah	8.0	90.9	2,749
Vermont	1.5	97.1	658
Virginia	4.7	72.5	8,388
Washington	8.9	84.8	7,960
West Virginia	1.1	95.6	1,852
Wisconsin	4.6	87.8	5,846
Wyoming	8.5	93.9	658

SOURCE: U.S. Bureau of the Census, Statistical Abstract of the United States, 1991, p. 22, table 27 (data from U.S. Bureau of the Census, Current Population Reports, Series P-25 and Census Press Release CB91-100). C 3.134:(year)
U.S. Bureau of the Census, Population Projections for States, by Age, Sex, Race, and Hispanic Origin: 1993 to 2020, tables 1 and 4. From Current Population Reports, P25-1111, downloaded from Census Bureau Bulletin Board. Telnet cenbbs.census.gov.

NOTES: 'Total' includes other races/ethnic groups not shown separately. 1990 data from the 1990 Census, 2000 data from projections by the US Bureau of the Census.

UNITS: Population in thousands of persons.

Chapter 2: Social Characteristics

Table 2.01 Marital Status, Persons 15 Years Old and Older, 1985, 1990, 1997

	Hispanic		White		Total	
	number	percent	number	percent	number	percent
1985						
All marital statuses	11,776	100.0%	157,090	100.0%	182,316	100.0%
single, never married	3,676	31.2	38,177	24.3	47,744	26.2
married, spouse present	6,036	51.3	92,465	58.9	102,229	56.1
married, spouse absent	782	6.6	3,960	2.5	5,770	3.2
widowed	553	4.7	11,404	7.3	13,484	7.4
divorced	729	6.2	11,084	7.1	13,089	7.2
1990						
All marital statuses	14,576	100.0%	163,417	100.0%	191,793	100.0%
single, never married	4,691	32.2	39,516	24.2	50,223	26.2
married, spouse present	7,363	50.5	95,337	58.3	106,513	55.3
married, spouse absent	1,022	7.0	4,191	2.6	6,118	3.2
widowed	548	3.8	11,731	7.2	13,810	7.2
divorced	952	6.5	12,643	7.7	15,128	7.9
1997						
All marital statuses	20,700	100.0%	173,296	100.0%	207,235	100.0%
single, never married	7,404	35.8	43,610	25.2	57,388	27.7
married, spouse present	9,729	47.0	96,790	55.9	109,331	52.8
married, spouse absent	1,401	6.8	5,057	2.9	7,420	3.6
widowed	721	3.5	11,668	6.7	13,749	6.6
divorced	1,444	7.0	16,171	9.3	19,347	9.3

SOURCE: U.S. Bureau of the Census, Current Population Reports: Marital Status and Living Arrangements, March, 1985, Series P-20, #410, p. 17, table 1; March, 1990, #450, p. 17, table 1; March, 1997(Update), #506, pp. 1-2, table 1. C3.186/6:(year); <www.census.gov/prod/3/98pubs/p20-506u.pdf>, accessed 15 October 1998.

NOTES: 'Total' includes other races and ethnic groups not shown separately.

UNITS: Number in thousands of persons 15 years old and older; percent as a percent of total (percents **not** standardized for age).

Table 2.02   Marital Status, Men 15 Years Old and Older, 1985, 1990, 1997

	Hispanic		White		Total	
	number	percent	number	percent	number	percent
Men:						
1985						
All marital statuses	5,809	100.0%	75,487	100.0%	87,034	100.0%
single, never married	2,125	36.6	21,276	28.2	26,108	30.0
married, spouse present	2,938	50.6	46,261	61.3	51,114	58.7
married, spouse absent	337	5.8	1,666	2.2	2,439	2.8
widowed	124	2.1	1,744	2.3	2,109	2.4
divorced	285	4.9	4,540	6.0	5,264	6.0
1990						
All marital statuses	7,254	100.0%	78,908	100.0%	91,033	100.0%
single, never married	2,674	36.9	22,078	28.0	27,422	30.1
married, spouse present	3,605	49.7	47,700	60.4	52,924	58.1
married, spouse absent	502	6.9	1,842	2.3	2,360	2.6
widowed	103	1.4	1,930	2.4	2,282	2.5
divorced	370	5.1	5,359	6.8	6,045	6.6
1997						
All marital statuses	10,627	100.0%	84,540	100.0%	100,159	100.0%
single, never married	4,354	41.0	24,471	28.9	31,315	31.3
married, spouse present	4,833	45.5	48,479	57.3	54,666	54.6
married, spouse absent	725	6.8	2,381	2.8	3,257	3.3
widowed	146	1.4	2,264	2.7	2,690	2.7
divorced	569	5.4	6,945	8.2	8,231	8.2

SOURCE: U.S. Bureau of the Census, Current Population Reports: Marital Status and Living Arrangements, March, 1985, Series P-20, #410, p. 17, table 1; March, 1990, #450, p. 17, table 1; March, 1997(Update), #506, pp. 1-2, table 1. C3.186/6:(year); <www.census.gov/prod/3/98pubs/p20-506u.pdf>, accessed 15 October 1998.

NOTES: 'Total' includes other races and ethnic groups not shown separately.

UNITS: Number in thousands of men 15 years old and older; percent as a percent of total (percents **not** standardized for age).

Table 2.03   Marital Status, Women 15 Years Old and Older, 1985, 1990, 1997

	Hispanic		White		Total	
	number	percent	number	percent	number	percent
Women:						
1985						
All marital statuses	5,967	100.0%	81,603	100.0%	95,282	100.0%
single, never married	1,551	26.0	16,901	20.7	21,636	22.7
married, spouse present	3,097	51.9	46,205	56.6	51,114	53.6
married, spouse absent	445	7.5	2,294	2.8	3,331	3.5
widowed	430	7.2	9,660	11.8	11,375	11.9
divorced	444	7.4	6,544	8.0	7,826	8.2
1990						
All marital statuses	7,323	100.0%	84,508	100.0%	99,838	100.0%
single, never married	2,017	27.5	17,438	20.6	22,718	22.8
married, spouse present	3,758	51.3	47,637	56.4	53,256	53.3
married, spouse absent	520	7.1	2,349	2.8	3,541	3.5
widowed	445	6.1	9,800	11.6	11,477	11.5
divorced	582	8.0	7,284	8.6	8,845	8.9
1997						
All marital statuses	10,073	100.0%	88,756	100.0%	107,076	100.0%
single, never married	3,050	30.3	19,139	21.6	26,073	24.4
married, spouse present	4,897	48.6	48,311	54.4	54,666	51.1
married, spouse absent	676	6.7	2,676	3.0	4,163	3.9
widowed	575	5.7	9,404	10.6	11,058	10.3
divorced	875	8.7	9,226	10.4	11,116	10.4

SOURCE: U.S. Bureau of the Census, <u>Current Population Reports: Marital Status and Living Arrangements, March, 1985</u>, Series P-20, #410, p. 17, table 1; <u>March, 1990</u>, #450, p: 17, table 1; <u>March, 1997(Update)</u>, #506, pp. 1-2, table 1. C3.186/6:(year); <www.census.gov/prod/3/98pubs/p20-506u.pdf>, accessed 15 October 1998.

NOTES: 'Total' includes other races and ethnic groups not shown separately.

UNITS: Number in thousands of women 15 years old and older; percent as a percent of total (percents **not** standardized for age).

Table 2.04 Marital Status of the Hispanic Population, by Type of Origin, 1985, 1990, 1997

	Mexican	Puerto Rican	Cuban	Central/ South Amer	other Hispanic	total Hispanic
1985						
Total population 15 years old and over						
number	6,814	1,774	867	1,280	1,040	11,776
percent	100.0%	100.0%	100.0%	100.0%	100.0%	100.0%
never married	31.0	37.5	19.7	32.7	29.9	31.2
married	59.6	50.1	63.1	58.4	55.2	57.9
widowed	4.0	4.2	8.8	3.8	7.5	4.7
divorced	5.4	8.2	8.4	5.1	7.4	6.2
1990						
Total population 15 years old and over						
number	8,943	1,523	846	2,156	1,109	14,576
percent	100.0%	100.0%	100.0%	100.0%	100.0%	100.0%
never married	33.1	34.9	20.0	33.0	28.2	32.2
married	57.8	52.3	62.8	58.3	57.3	57.5
widowed	3.4	4.5	7.1	2.8	5.2	3.8
divorced	5.7	8.3	10.0	5.8	9.3	6.5
1997						
Total population 15 years old and over						
number	12,598	2,199	1,054	3,250	1,598	20,700
percent	100.0%	100.0%	100.0%	100.0%	100.0%	100.0%
never married	35.4	39.0	23.8	38.5	36.8	35.8
married	56.0	45.7	57.3	52.4	47.5	53.8
widowed	2.9	4.1	7.2	3.5	5.1	3.5
divorced	5.8	11.2	11.7	5.5	10.6	7.0

SOURCE: U.S. Bureau of the Census, The Hispanic Population in the United States: March, 1985, pp. 12-13, table 1 (data from U.S. Bureau of the Census, *Current Population Reports*). C 3.186:P-20/422

U.S. Bureau of the Census, The Hispanic Population in the United States: March, 1990, pp. 6-7, table 1; (data from U.S. Bureau of the Census, *Current Population Reports*). C 3.186/14-2:990

U.S. Census Bureau, "Hispanic Population of the United States, (Table 8.1). March, 1997 CPS: Marital Status by Race-Ethnicity Age 15 and over: Both Sexes - Values/Percents;" released 7 August 1998; <http://www.census.gov/population/socdemo/hispanic/cps97/tab08-1.txt>

NOTES: Total population includes other races and ethnic groups not shown separately. 'Other Hispanic origin' includes persons from Spain and persons identifying themselves generally as Hispanic, Spanish, Spanish-American, Hispano, Latino, etc.

UNITS: Total resident population in thousands of persons 15 years old and over; percent as a percent of total shown (100.0%).

Table 2.05 Race and Hispanic Origin of Husbands and Wives, March, 1997

	race of the wife			origin of the wife		
	White	Black	other	His-panic origin	other origin	Total
Race of the husband:						
Total	48,311	3,809	2,545	4,897	49,769	54,666
White	47,791	110	577	4,696	43,783	48,479
Black	201	3,698	56	116	3,839	3,955
other	319	1	1,912	85	2,147	2,232
Origin of the husband:						
Total	48,311	3,809	2,545	4,897	49,769	54,666
Hispanic origin	4,626	99	107	4,034	799	4,833
other origin	43,685	3,710	2,439	863	48,970	49,833

SOURCE: U.S. Bureau of the Census, Current Population Reports: Household and Family Characteristics: March, 1997, Series P-20, #509, p. 131, table 13. C 3.186/6:997

NOTES: Total population includes other races and ethnic groups not shown separately.

UNITS: All married couples in thousands couples.

Table 2.06 Hispanic Married Couple Households, by Type of Origin of the Husband and Wife, 1993

| | origin of the wife | | | | | |
	Mex-ican	Puerto Rican	Cuban	Central/ South Amer	other Hispanic	total Hispanic
By origin of the wife:						
Total population	100.0%	100.0%	100.0%	100.0%	100.0%	100.0%
total Hispanic population	85.1	81.4	82.9	84.4	65.7	83.1
by origin						
Mexican origin	82.8	2.7	1.7	4.3	1.4	53.6
Puerto Rican origin	0.1	70.7	2.1	2.1	1.4	6.7
Cuban origin	0.1	1.2	77.1	2.8	0.7	5.5
Central/South American origin	1.6	3.7	1.3	74.8	2.1	12.1
other Hispanic origin	0.5	3.0	0.8	0.4	60.1	5.2
not of Hispanic origin	14.9	18.6	17.1	15.6	34.3	16.9
By origin of the husband:						
Total population	4.5%	0.6%	0.4%	1.0%	0.5%	7.1%
total Hispanic population	55.7	7.3	5.4	12.3	5.1	85.8
by origin						
Mexican origin	85.6	0.4	0.2	1.0	0.2	87.3
Puerto Rican origin	0.9	69.3	1.5	3.3	1.2	76.1
Cuban origin	1.3	1.7	79.7	6.5	0.9	90.1
Central/South American origin	7.4	2.3	0.6	77.4	1.2	88.9
other Hispanic origin	4.2	3.8	0.8	0.8	64.9	74.4
not of Hispanic origin	0.7	0.1	0.1	0.2	0.2	1.3

SOURCE: U.S. Bureau of the Census, The Hispanic Population in the United States: March, 1993, p. 6, table A (data from U.S. Bureau of the Census, *Current Population Reports*). C 3.186/14-2:993

NOTES: Total population includes other races and ethnic groups not shown separately. 'Other Hispanic origin' includes persons from Spain and persons identifying themselves generally as Hispanic, Spanish, Spanish-American, Hispano, Latino, etc.

UNITS: Percent as a percent of total shown (100.0%).

Table 2.07 Age, Educational Attainment, and Residence, 1985

	Hispanic	White	Total
Age			
Persons of all ages	16,940	199,117	234,066
persons:			
under 5 years old	1,809	14,610	17,958
5-14 years old	3,355	27,417	33,792
15-44 years old	8,540	93,852	110,948
45-64 years old	2,407	39,033	44,549
65 years old and over	819	24,205	26,818
Years of school completed			
All persons 25 years old and over	8,455	124,905	143,524
persons completing:			
0-8 years of school	3,192	16,224	19,893
1-3 years high school	1,210	14,365	17,553
4 years high school	2,402	48,728	54,866
1-3 years college	932	20,652	23,405
4 or more years college	718	24,935	27,808
Residence			
Northeast	3,144	43,185	49,276
Midwest	1,389	52,280	58,587
South	5,288	63,155	79,165
West	6,964	40,394	46,489
nonfarm	na	na	na
farm	na	na	na
inside metro areas	na	na	na
outside metro areas	na	na	na

SOURCE: U.S. Bureau of the Census, Statistical Abstract of the United States, 1987, p. 35, table 39, (data from U.S. Bureau of the Census, *Current Population Reports*, Series P-25). C 3.134:987
U.S. Bureau of the Census, Current Population Reports: Money Income of Households, Families and Persons in the United States, 1984, Series P-60 (#151), pp. 10-17, table 4. C3.186/22:984

NOTES: 'Total' includes other races and ethnic groups not shown separately.

UNITS: Population in thousands of persons; percent distribution as a percent of total, 100.0%.

Table 2.08   Age, Educational Attainment, and Residence, 1990

	Hispanic	White	Total
Age			
Persons of all ages			
persons:	21,405	208,611	248,644
under 18 years old	7,457	51,929	65,049
18-24 years old	2,741	20,383	24,901
25-44 years old	7,139	68,807	81,570
45-64 years old	2,977	40,594	47,032
65 years old and over	1,091	26,898	30,093
Years of school completed			
All persons 25 years old			
and over	11,208	136,299	158,694
persons that:			
did not complete high school	5,455	27,409	34,228
completed high school,			
no college	3,285	53,250	61,272
completed some college, not			
a college graduate	1,379	25,358	29,169
completed college	1,088	30,283	34,025
Residence			
Northeast	3,531	43,727	50,799
Midwest	1,399	52,771	59,914
South	6,598	66,492	85,097
West	9,878	45,622	52,835
nonfarm	21,297	204,001	243,865
farm	108	4,610	4,779
inside metro areas	19,883	159,443	193,052
outside metro areas	1,522	49,168	55,592

SOURCE: U.S. Bureau of the Census, <u>Current Population Reports: Poverty in the United States: 1990</u>, Series P-60, #175, p. 24, table 5; pp. 84-87, table 11; p. 154, table 21. C3.186/11:990

NOTES: 'Total' includes other races and ethnic groups not shown separately.

UNITS: Population in thousands of persons; percent distribution as a percent of total, 100.0%.

Table 2.09   Age and Residence, 1997

	Hispanic	White	Total
Age			
Persons of all ages			
persons:	30,637	221,200	268,480
under 18 years old	10,802	55,863	71,069
18-24 years old	3,791	20,259	25,201
25-34 years old	5,488	31,778	39,354
35-44 years old	4,606	36,736	44,462
45-54 years old	2,700	28,871	34,057
55-59 years old	930	10,458	12,190
60-64 years old	703	8,681	10,065
65 years old and over	1,617	28,553	32,082
Residence			
Northeast	4,821	42,997	51,202
Midwest	2,276	54,737	62,498
South	9,897	72,717	94,235
West	13,644	50,749	60,545
inside metro areas	27,761	175,164	216,143
outside metro areas	2,876	46,037	52,337

SOURCE: U.S. Bureau of the Census, <u>Current Population Reports: Poverty in the United States: 1997</u>, Series P-60, #201, pp. 2-5, table 2; pp. 24-26, table 5. <www.census.gov/prod/3/98pubs/p60-201.pdf>, accessed 15 October 1998.

NOTES: 'Total' includes other races and ethnic groups not shown separately.

UNITS: Population in thousands of persons.

Chapter 3:
Household & Family Characteristics

Table 3.01   Selected Characteristics of Households, 1985

	Hispanic	White	Total
Marital status and sex of the householder			
All households, both sexes	4,883	75,328	86,789
male householder	3,357	53,868	60,025
married, wife present	2,638	43,444	47,683
married, wife absent	129	1,013	1,416
widowed	84	1,386	1,620
divorced	162	3,078	3,535
single, never married	344	4,947	5,772
female householder	1,526	21,461	26,763
married, husband present	186	2,199	2,667
married, husband absent	351	1,668	2,497
widowed	313	8,304	9,728
divorced	334	5,203	6,265
single, never married	342	4,087	5,606
Age of the householder			
All ages	4,883	75,328	86,789
15-24 years old	489	4,626	5,438
25-34 years old	1,363	17,010	20,013
35-44 years old	1,184	15,024	17,481
45-54 years old	743	10,792	12,628
55-64 years old	606	11,471	13,073
65 years old and over	497	16,406	18,155
Housing tenure			
All tenures	4,883	75,328	86,789
own housing unit	2,007	50,611	55,845
rent housing unit	2,876	24,667	30,943

continued on the next page

Table 3.01   continued

	Hispanic	White	Total
Size of the household			
All household sizes	4,883	75,328	86,789
one person	756	17,876	20,602
two persons	1,026	24,558	27,289
three persons	995	13,336	15,465
four persons	959	11,795	13,631
five persons	576	5,061	6,108
six persons	297	1,819	2,299
seven or more persons	275	882	1,296
persons per household	2.96	2.64	2.69
Residence			
All residences	4,883	75,328	86,789
Northeast	1,017	16,244	18,348
Midwest	376	19,599	21,697
South	1,553	24,283	29,581
West	1,937	15,202	17,163
inside metropolitan areas	na	na	na
outside metropolitan areas	na	na	na
nonfarm	na	na	na
farm	na	na	na

SOURCE: U.S. Bureau of the Census, <u>Current Population Reports: Money Income of Households Families and Persons in the United States; March 1984</u>, Series P-60, #151, pp. 10-14, table 4. C3.186/2:984
U.S. Bureau of the Census, <u>Current Population Reports: Household & Family Characteristics, March 1985</u>, Series P-20, #411, pp. 107-112, table 22. C3.186/17:985

NOTES: 'Total' includes other races and ethnic groups not shown separately.

UNITS: Number of households in thousands of households; persons per household, average.

Table 3.02 Selected Characteristics of Households, 1990

	Hispanic	White	Total
Marital status and sex of the householder			
All households, both sexes	5,933	80,163	93,347
family households	4,840	56,590	66,090
married couple families	3,395	46,981	52,317
male householder, no wife present	329	2,303	2,884
female householder, no husband present	1,116	7,306	10,890
non-family households	1,093	23,573	27,257
male householder	587	9,951	11,606
-living alone	415	7,718	9,049
female householder	506	13,622	15,651
-living alone	442	12,161	13,950
Age of the householder			
All ages	5,933	80,163	93,347
15-24 years old	542	4,222	5,121
25-34 years old	1,721	17,137	20,472
35-44 years old	1,405	17,395	20,554
45-54 years old	930	12,404	14,514
55-64 years old	664	10,862	12,529
65 years old and over	671	18,144	20,156
Housing tenure			
All tenures	5,933	80,163	93,347
own housing unit	2,443	54,094	59,846
rent housing unit	3,383	24,685	31,895

continued on the next page

Table 3.02   continued

	Hispanic	White	Total
Size of the household			
All household sizes	5,933	80,163	93,347
one person	856	19,879	22,999
two persons	1,292	26,714	30,114
three persons	1,139	13,585	16,128
four persons	1,172	12,399	14,456
five persons	752	5,104	6,213
six persons	386	1,615	2,143
seven or more persons	336	877	1,295
persons per household	3.48	2.58	2.63
Residence			
All residences	5,933	80,163	93,347
Northeast	1,037	16,773	19,127
Midwest	398	20,339	22,760
South	1,953	26,155	32,262
West	2,544	16,896	19,197
inside metropolitan areas	5,479	61,155	72,331
outside metropolitan areas	454	19,009	21,016
nonfarm	8,897	78,556	91,710
farm	36	1,608	1,637

SOURCE: U.S. Bureau of the Census, Current Population Reports: Money Income of Households Families and Persons in the United States: 1988 and 1989, Series P-60, #172, pp. 9-12, table 1. C3.186/2:989

NOTES: 'Total' includes other races and ethnic groups not shown separately.

UNITS: Number of households in thousands of households; persons per household, average.

Table 3.03   Selected Characteristics of Households, 1997

	Hispanic	White	Total
Marital status and type of householder			
All households, both sexes	8,590	86,106	102,528
family households	6,961	59,511	70,880
married couple families	4,804	48,066	54,317
male householder, no wife present	545	3,137	3,911
female householder, no husband present	1,612	8,308	12,652
non-family households	1,630	26,596	31,648
male householder	875	11,725	14,133
-living alone	623	9,018	11,010
female householder	754	14,871	17,516
-living alone	617	12,980	15,317
Age of the householder			
All ages	8,590	86,106	102,528
15-24 years old	780	4,242	5,435
25-34 years old	2,303	15,344	19,033
35-44 years old	2,316	19,761	23,943
45-54 years old	1,386	16,400	19,547
55-64 years old	889	11,163	13,072
65 years old and over	916	19,196	21,497
Housing tenure			
All tenures	8,590	86,106	102,528
own housing unit	3,857	60,050	67,873
rent housing unit	4,571	24,635	32,954

continued on the next page

Table 3.03   continued

	Hispanic	White	Total
Size of the household			
All household sizes	8,590	86,106	102,528
one person	1,240	21,998	26,327
two persons	1,838	28,817	32,965
three persons	1,728	14,215	17,331
four persons	1,763	12,654	15,358
five persons	1,199	5,801	7,048
six persons	463	1,738	2,232
seven or more persons	358	883	1,267
Residence			
All residences	8,590	86,106	102,528
Northeast	1,468	16,926	19,810
Midwest	644	21,465	24,236
South	2,939	28,948	36,578
West	3,539	18,767	21,905
inside metropolitan areas	7,808	67,800	82,122
outside metropolitan areas	783	18,307	20,406

SOURCE: U.S. Bureau of the Census, Current Population Reports: Money Income in the United States: 1997, Series P-60, #200, pp. 1-4, table 1.
<www.census.gov/prod/3/98pubs/p60-200.pdf> accessed 15 October 1998

NOTES: 'Total' includes other races and ethnic groups not shown separately.

UNITS: Number of households in thousands of households.

Table 3.04 Type, Size, and Tenure of Hispanic Households, by Type of Hispanic Origin, 1997

			type of origin			
	Mexican	Puerto Rican	Cuban	Central/ South Amer	other Hispanic	total Hispanic
All households						
number	4,830	1,043	496	1,164	691	8,225
percent	100.0%	100.0%	100.0%	100.0%	100.0%	100.0%
percent by type-						
family households	83.0%	74.8%	73.8%	82.7%	74.5%	80.6%
non-family households	17.0	25.2	26.2	17.3	25.5	19.4
male householder	6.4	4.7	4.6	6.7	5.3	6.0
female householder	16.7	29.5	12.5	22.1	26.5	19.7
percent by size-						
one person	12.4%	20.1%	21.2%	12.2%	20.0%	14.5%
two persons	20.1	23.5	34.1	22.6	24.2	22.1
three persons	18.8	20.8	21.0	21.6	24.4	20.1
four persons	20.2	20.4	14.9	21.4	17.9	19.8
five persons	13.8	9.1	5.4	13.0	7.9	12.1
six persons	8.2	3.7	2.2	5.8	3.3	6.5
seven or more persons	6.5	2.4	1.3	3.4	2.3	4.9
percent by tenure-						
own (or buying) home	46.3%	30.8%	55.2%	34.3%	45.0%	43.1%
rent home	51.7	67.8	43.6	65.1	52.6	55.2

SOURCE: U.S. Census Bureau, "Hispanic Population of the United States, (Table 6.1). March, 1997 CPS: Type of Household by Race-Ethnicity: (Detailed Categories) - Values/Percent;"; "Hispanic Population of the United States, (Table 6.2). March, 1997 CPS: Type of Household by Race-Ethnicity: (Collapsed Categories) - Values/Percent;"; "Hispanic Population of the United States, (Table 6.3). March, 1997 CPS: Tenure of Household by Race-Ethnicity: - Values/Percent;"; "Hispanic Population of the United States, (Table 6.6). March, 1997 CPS: Number of persons in Household by Race-Ethnicity: - Values/Percent;" released 7 August 1998; < http://www.census.gov/population/socdemo/hispanic/cps97/tab06-1.txt > < http://www.census.gov/population/socdemo/hispanic/cps97/tab06-2.txt > < http://www.census.gov/population/socdemo/hispanic/cps97/tab06-3.txt > < http://www.census.gov/population/socdemo/hispanic/cps97/tab06-6.txt >

NOTES: Total population includes other races and ethnic groups not shown separately. 'Other Hispanic origin' includes persons from Spain and persons identifying themselves generally as Hispanic, Spanish, Spanish-American, Hispano, Latino, etc.

UNITS: Households in thousands of households; percent as a percent of all households by type (100.0%).

Table 3.05   Selected Characteristics of Family Households, 1985

	Hispanic	White	Total
Type of family			
All families	3,939	54,400	62,706
married couple families	2,824	45,643	50,350
male householder,			
no wife present	210	1,816	2,228
female householder,			
no husband present	905	6,941	10,129
Size of family			
All family sizes	3,939	54,400	62,706
two persons	962	22,711	25,349
three persons	948	12,743	14,804
four persons	936	11,517	13,259
five persons	552	4,894	5,894
six persons	276	1,704	2,175
seven or more persons	266	831	1,225
average per family	3.88	3.16	3.23
Number of related children			
under 18 years old			
All families	3,939	54,400	62,706
no children	1,337	28,169	31,594
one child	904	11,174	13,108
two children	865	9,937	11,645
three children	481	3,695	4,486
four children	215	1,049	1,329
five children	87	261	373
six or more children	50	115	171
average per family	1.44	0.88	0.92
average per family			
with children	2.18	1.83	1.85

continued on the next page

Hispanic Americans: A Statistical Sourcebook

Table 3.05   continued

	Hispanic	White	Total
Number of earners			
All families	3,905	53,777	61,930
no earner	599	7,674	9,221
one earner	1,290	15,219	17,949
two earners	1,485	23,303	26,160
three earners	370	5,317	6,029
four earners or more	161	2,263	2,570
Housing tenure			
All tenures	3,939	54,400	62,706
own housing unit	1,772	40,865	45,015
rent housing unit	2,167	13,535	17,691
Residence			
All residences	3,939	54,400	62,706
Northeast	808	11,631	13,149
Midwest	313	14,309	15,839
South	1,273	17,953	21,781
West	1,545	10,507	11,938
nonfarm	na	na	na
farm	na	na	na
inside metropolitan areas	na	na	na
outside metropolitan areas	na	na	na

SOURCE: U.S. Bureau of the Census, <u>Current Population Reports: Money Income of Households, Families, and Persons in the United States, 1984</u>, Series P-60, #151, pp. 76-77, table 21. C3.186/2:984
U.S. Bureau of the Census, <u>Current Population Reports: Household & Family Characteristics, March 1985</u>, Series P-20, #437, pp. 13-45, table 1; pp. 107-111, table 22. C3.186/17:985

NOTES: 'Total' includes other races and ethnic groups not shown separately. 'Number of earners' excludes families with members in the armed forces.

UNITS: Number of households in thousands of family households.

Table 3.06   Selected Characteristics of Family Households, 1990

	Hispanic	White	Total
Type of family			
All families	4,840	56,590	66,090
married couple families	3,395	46,981	52,317
male householder, no			
wife present	329	2,303	2,884
female householder, no			
husband present	1,116	7,306	10,890
Size of family			
All family sizes	4,840	56,590	66,090
two persons	1,226	24,438	27,606
three persons	1,114	12,937	15,353
four persons	1,146	12,048	14,036
five persons	714	4,882	5,938
six persons	347	1,505	1,997
seven or more persons	293	781	1,170
average per family	3.83	3.11	3.17
Number of related children			
under 18 years old			
All families	4,840	56,590	66,090
no children	1,790	29,872	33,801
one child	1,095	11,186	13,530
two children	1,036	10,342	12,263
three children	579	3,853	4,650
four children	232	970	1,279
five children	73	247	379
six or more children	35	121	188
average per family	1.34	0.86	0.89
average per family			
with children	2.12	1.82	1.83

continued on the next page

Table 3.06   continued

	Hispanic	White	Total
Number of earners			
All families	4,840	56,590	66,090
no earner	615	7,816	9,439
one earner	1,554	14,970	18,146
two earners	1,860	25,737	29,235
three earners	541	5,832	6,724
four earners or more	271	2,236	2,546
Housing tenure			
All tenures	4,840	56,590	66,090
own housing unit	3,448	42,588	47,142
rent housing unit	2,678	14,003	18,948
Residence			
All residences	4,840	56,590	66,090
Northeast	815	11,837	13,494
Midwest	330	14,370	16,059
South	1,596	18,746	23,244
West	2,101	11,638	13,293
nonfarm	4,813	55,225	64,701
farm	28	1,365	1,390
inside metropolitan areas	6,256	42,592	50,619
outside metropolitan areas	1,215	13,999	15,471

SOURCE: U.S. Bureau of the Census, <u>Current Population Reports: Money Income of Households, Families, and Persons in the United States: 1988 and 1989</u>, Series P-60, #172, pp. 9-11, table 1; pp. 48-50, table 13; pp. 76-80, table 18. C3.186/2:989
U.S. Bureau of the Census, <u>Current Population Reports: Household & Family Characteristics: March 1990 and 1989</u>, Series P-20, #447, pp. 13-16, table 1; pp. 18-20, table 2. C3.186/17:989

NOTES: 'Total' includes other races and ethnic groups not shown separately.
'Number of earners' excludes families with members in the armed forces.

UNITS: Number of households in thousands of family households.

Table 3.07   Selected Characteristics of Family Households, 1997

	Hispanic	White	Total
Type of family			
All families	6,961	59,515	70,884
married couple families	4,804	48,070	54,321
male householder, no			
wife present	545	3,137	3,911
female householder, no			
husband present	1,612	8,308	12,652
Size of family			
All family sizes	6,961	59,515	70,884
two persons	1,748	26,380	30,287
three persons	1,669	13,312	16,231
four persons	1,678	12,078	14,633
five persons	1,108	5,366	6,555
six persons	445	1,598	2,047
seven or more persons	313	782	1,130

continued on the next page

Table 3.07   continued

	Hispanic	White	Total
Number of earners			
All families	6,961	59,515	70,884
no earner	815	8,367	9,835
one earner	2,434	16,239	20,494
two earners	2,761	27,467	31,752
three earners	669	5,618	6,638
four earners or more	282	1,824	2,165
Residence			
All residences	6,961	59,515	70,884
Northeast	1,128	11,390	13,338
Midwest	542	14,771	16,594
South	2,341	20,358	25,682
West	2,950	12,996	15,270
inside metropolitan areas	6,307	46,429	56,350
outside metropolitan areas	654	13,086	14,534

SOURCE: U.S. Bureau of the Census, Current Population Reports: Money Income in the United States: 1997, Series P-60, #200, pp 13-16, table 4. <www.census.gov/prod/3/98pubs/p60-200.pdf>, accessed 15 October 1998.

NOTES: 'Total' includes other races and ethnic groups not shown separately. 'Number of earners' excludes families with members in the armed forces.

UNITS: Number of households in thousands of family households.

Table 3.08 Type and Size of Hispanic Family Households, by Type of Hispanic Origin, 1997

	type of origin					
	Mexican	Puerto Rican	Cuban	Central/ South Amer	other Hispanic	total Hispanic
All family households	100.0%	100.0%	100.0%	100.0%	100.0%	100.0%
married couple families	72.2	54.3	76.9	65.2	57.3	68.2
female householder	20.2	39.4	16.9	26.8	35.5	24.4
male householder	7.7	6.3	6.2	8.0	7.1	7.4
two persons	23.5	29.1	41.8	26.5	29.6	26.1
three persons	21.5	27.2	27.4	24.9	30.5	23.7
four persons	23.1	25.7	19.5	25.1	22.5	23.5
five persons	15.8	10.7	7.3	13.8	10.7	14.0
six persons	9.0	4.9	2.2	6.3	3.6	7.4
seven or more persons	7.0	2.4	1.8	3.4	3.0	5.4

Source: U.S. Census Bureau, "Hispanic Population of the United States, (Table 4.1). March, 1997 CPS: Type of Family by Race-Ethnicity - Values/Percents;" "Hispanic Population of the United States, (Table 4.2). March, 1997 CPS: Size of Family by Race-Ethnicity - Values/Percents;" released 7 August 1998; <http://www.census.gov/population/socdemo/hispanic/cps97/tab04-1.txt> <http://www.census.gov/population/socdemo/hispanic/cps97/tab04-2.txt>

NOTES: Total population includes other races and ethnic groups not shown separately. 'Other Hispanic origin' includes persons from Spain and persons identifying themselves generally as Hispanic, Spanish, Spanish-American, Hispano, Latino, etc.

UNITS: Family households by type as a percent of all households as shown (100.0%).

Table 3.09 Families With Own Children Under 18 Years Old, 1985, 1990, 1997

	Hispanic families	White families	All families
1985			
Total	3,939	54,400	62,706
all families with own children under 18 years old	2,602	26,232	31,112
- married couple families	1,892	21,565	24,210
- male householder families	68	744	896
- female householder families	642	3,922	6,006
all families with own children under 6 years old	1,386	11,937	14,202
- married couple families	1,081	10,410	11,715
- male householder families	17	211	276
- female householder families	288	1,315	2,210
all families with own children under 3 years old	839	7,290	8,503
- married couple families	667	6,550	7,295
- male householder families	9	101	136
- female householder families	162	639	1,073
1990			
Total	4,840	56,950	66,090
all families with own children under 18 years old	3,051	26,718	32,289
- married couple families	2,188	21,579	24,537
- male householder families	118	939	1,153
- female householder families	745	4,199	6,599
all families with own children under 6 years old	1,633	12,516	15,186
- married couple families	1,226	10,616	12,051
- male householder families	64	335	436
- female householder families	343	1,565	2,699
all families with own children under 3 years old	978	7,493	9,055
- married couple families	729	6,486	7,331
- male householder families	42	211	276
- female householder families	207	795	1,447

continued on the next page

Table 3.09   continued

	Hispanic families	White families	All families
1997			
Total	6,631	58,934	70,241
all families with own children under			
18 years old	4,305	28,236	34,665
- married couple families	2,962	21,914	25,083
- male householder families	204	1,325	1,709
- female householder families	1,138	4,997	7,874
all families with own children under			
6 years old	2,278	12,551	15,394
- married couple families	1,649	10,169	11,585
- male householder families	127	545	715
- female householder families	502	1,837	3,095
all families with own children under			
3 years old	1,362	7,217	8,761
- married couple families	990	6,066	6,838
- male householder families	82	304	411
- female householder families	290	848	1,511

SOURCE: U.S. Bureau of the Census, <u>Current Population Reports: Household & Family Characteristics, March, 1985</u>, Series P-20, #441, pp. 13-14, table 1; <u>March, 1990 and 1989</u>, Series P-20, #447, pp. 13-16, table 1; C3.186/17:(year); <u>March, 1997</u> Series P-20, #509, pp. 1-5, table 1. <www.census.gov/prod/3/98pubs/p20-509u.pdf>, accessed 15 October 1998. C3.186/17:(year)

NOTES: 'All families' includes families of other races and ethnic groups not shown separately.

UNITS: Thousands of family households.

Table 3.10 Living Arrangements of Children Under 18 Years of Age by Selected Characteristic of the Parent, 1985, 1990, 1997

	Hispanic children	White children	All children
1985			
All children living with one or both parents	5,856	49,829	60,784
children living with both parents	4,110	40,690	46,149
- parents high school graduates	45.8%	82.2%	81.3%
- at least one parent employed	3,322	36,075	40,306
-- both parents employed	1,451	19,872	22,595
children living with mother only	1,612	7,929	13,081
- mother high school graduate	34.2%	66.4%	64.7%
- mother employed	573	4,553	6,675
-- mother employed full time	441	3,539	5,227
children living with father only	134	1,210	1,554
- father high school graduate	63.0%	77.6%	75.0%
- father employed	105	976	1,199
-- father employed full time	90	901	1,089
1990			
All children living with one or both parents	6,943	50,462	62,370
children living with both parents	4,789	40,593	46,503
- parents high school graduates	48.4%	84.5%	83.9%
- at least one parent employed	3,883	35,953	40,564
-- both parents employed	1,942	22,459	25,669
children living with mother only	1,943	8,321	13,874
- mother high school graduate	43.8%	72.2%	69.4%
- mother employed	832	5,050	7,646
-- mother employed full time	607	3,992	6,106
children living with father only	211	1,549	1,993
- father high school graduate	51.5%	74.6%	73.6%
- father employed	168	1,262	1,565
-- father employed full time	158	1,165	1,445

continued on the next page

Table 3.10   continued

	Hispanic children	White children	All children
1997			
All children living with one or both parents	10,008	54,198	68,185
children living with both parents	6,748	41,654	48,386
- parents high school graduates	1,687	12,453	14,653
- at least one parent employed	5,240	35,553	41,027
-- both parents employed	2,965	25,004	28,936
children living with mother only	2,819	10,204	16,740
- mother high school graduate	758	3,830	6,228
- mother employed	1,360	6,840	10,505
-- mother employed full time	1,018	5,270	8,250
children living with father only	441	2,339	3,059
- father high school graduate	125	893	1,252
- father employed	361	1,929	2,456
-- father employed full time	333	1,793	2,297

SOURCE: U.S. Bureau of the Census, Current Population Reports: Marital Status and Living Arrangements: March, 1985 Series P-20, #410, pp. 51-62, table 9; March, 1990, Series P-20, #450, pp. 45-56, table 6; C3.186/6:(year); March, 1997(Update), Series P-20, #506, pp. 36-45, table 6. <www.census.gov/prod/3/98pubs/p20-506u.pdf>, accessed 15 October 1998.

NOTES: 'All children' includes children of other races and ethnic groups not shown separately.

UNITS: Thousands of children living in family households.
'Parents/Mother/Father high school graduates': percent as a percent of all children living with parents/mother/father (100%)

Table 3.11 Primary Child Care Arrangements Used for Preschoolers by Families With Employed Mothers, Fall 1994

	Hispanic children	White children	All children
All preschoolers	1,205	8,587	10,288
Care in child's home by:			
Father	204	1,663	1,898
Grandparent	96	460	604
Other relative	88	258	355
Non-relative	69	479	524
Care in another home by:			
Grandparent	174	834	1,068
Other relative	111	433	565
Non-relative	181	1,366	1,586
Organized facilities:			
Daycare center	154	1,879	2,218
Nursery/preschool	78	624	801
Mother cares for child	26	518	563

SOURCE: U.S. Bureau of the Census, Current Population Reports: Who's Minding our Preshcoolers? Fall, 1994(Update) Series P70-62, p. 1, table 1. C3.186/P70-62

NOTES: 'All children' includes children of other races and ethnic groups not shown separately.

UNITS: Thousands of children living in family households.

Chapter 4: Education - Preprimary through High School

Table 4.01 School Enrollment by Age, 1985, 1991, 1996

	enrollment			enrollment rate		
	Hispanic	White	Total	Hispanic	White	Total
1985						
all persons 3-34 years old	5.1	47.5	58.0	47.7%	47.8%	48.3%
persons 3 and 4 years old	0.2	2.3	2.8	27.0	38.6	38.9
persons 5 and 6 years old	0.7	5.4	6.7	94.5	96.4	96.1
persons 7-13 years old	2.3	18.5	22.8	99.0	99.3	99.2
persons 14 and 15 years old	0.6	6.0	7.4	96.1	98.1	98.1
persons 16 and 17 years old	0.6	5.4	6.7	84.5	91.6	91.7
persons 18 and 19 years old	0.2	3.1	3.7	41.8	52.4	51.6
persons 20 and 21 years old	0.1	2.3	2.7	24.0	36.1	35.3
persons 22-24 years old	0.1	1.7	2.1	11.6	17.0	16.9
persons 25-29 years old	0.1	1.6	1.9	6.6	9.2	9.2
persons 30-34 years old	0.1	1.0	1.2	5.7	6.2	6.1
persons 35 years old and older	na	1.5	1.8	na	1.7	1.7
1991						
all persons 3-34 years old	6,306	49,156	61,276	47.9%	50.0%	50.7%
persons 3 and 4 years old	299	2,502	3,068	30.6	41.3	40.5
persons 5 and 6 years old	850	5,727	7,178	92.4	95.3	95.4
persons 7-9 years old	1,333	8,825	11,022	99.9	99.6	99.6
persons 10-13 years old	1,576	11,500	14,423	99.4	99.7	99.7
persons 14 and 15 years old	732	5,311	6,634	97.2	98.7	98.8
persons 16 and 17 years old	532	4,902	6,155	82.6	93.3	93.3
persons 18 and 19 years old	394	3,197	3,969	47.9	59.7	59.6
persons 20 and 21 years old	215	2,517	3,041	26.4	43.2	42.0
persons 22-24 years old	144	1,910	2,365	11.6	21.7	22.2
persons 25-29 years old	140	1,646	2,045	6.9	9.9	10.2
persons 30-34 years old	93	1,119	1,377	4.5	6.0	6.2
persons 35 years old and old	148	2,219	2,620	2.0	2.2	2.2

continued on the next page

Table 4.01   continued

1996	enrollment			enrollment rate		
	Hispanic	White	Total	Hispanic	White	Total
all persons 3-34 years old	8,570	52,987	67,317	50.3%	53.4%	54.1%
persons 3 and 4 years old	502	3,052	3,959	38.1	47.9	48.3
persons 5 and 6 years old	1,188	6,215	7,893	89.5	94.8	94.0
persons 7-9 years old	1,588	9,042	11,577	96.6	97.1	97.2
persons 10-13 years old	2,122	12,133	15,359	97.6	98.2	98.1
persons 14 and 15 years old	978	5,997	7,598	96.6	98.0	98.0
persons 16 and 17 years old	862	5,680	7,220	88.7	92.8	92.8
persons 18 and 19 years old	470	3,645	4,539	47.0	62.5	61.5
persons 20 and 21 years old	244	2,428	3,017	25.3	44.9	44.4
persons 22-24 years old	272	2,070	2,605	17.6	24.6	24.8
persons 25-29 years old	217	1,741	2,265	8.6	11.3	11.9
persons 30-34 years old	127	984	1,286	5.0	5.7	6.1
persons 35 years old and over	248	2,392	2,979	2.5	2.2	2.3

SOURCE: U.S. Bureau of the Census, Statistical Abstract of the United States, 1988, p. 122, table 196 (data from *Current Population Reports*, Series P-20). C 3.134:(year)

U.S. Bureau of the Census, Current Population Reports: School Enrollment-Social and Economic Characteristics of Students: October 1991, Series P-20, #469, pp. 1-2, table 1; C3.186/12:99(year) October, 1996 (Update), #500, pp. 1-2, table 1, <www.census.gov/prod/3/98pubs/p20-500u.pdf>, accessed 15 October 1998.

NOTES: 'Total' includes other races and ethnic groups not shown separately.

UNITS: 1985 data: Enrollment in millions of persons enrolled; 1991 & 1996 data: enrollment in thousands of persons enrolled. All years: rate as a percent of the civilian non-institutionalized population, by age group.

Table 4.02 School Enrollment by Level and Control of School, 1985, 1991, 1996

	Hispanic	White	Total
1985			
Total enrolled	5,070	47,452	58,014
nursery school	168	2,087	2,491
public	105	617	854
private	63	1,470	1,637
kindergarten	364	3,060	3,815
public	315	2,545	3,221
private	49	515	594
elementary school	2,083	21,593	26,866
public	2,608	18,817	23,803
private	196	2,776	3,063
high school	1,156	11,378	13,979
public	1,090	10,258	12,764
private	167	1,120	1,215
college	579	9,334	10,863
public	464	7,131	8,379
private	116	2,203	2,483
1991			
Total enrolled	6,306	49,156	61,276
nursery school	215	2,447	2,933
public	146	810	1,094
private	69	1,637	1,839
kindergarten	552	3,274	4,152
public	525	2,766	3,531
private	27	508	621
elementary school	3,461	23,547	29,591
public	3,240	20,948	26,632
private	221	2,599	2,958
high school	1,357	10,309	13,010
public	1,299	9,467	12,069
private	61	841	945
college	721	9,579	11,589
public	607	7,464	9,078
private	115	2,118	2,511
college full time	481	6,919	8,461

continued on the next page

Table 4.02   continued

	Hispanic	White	Total
1996			
Total enrolled	7,497	42,971	54,762
public	6,927	36,483	47,203
private	570	6,489	7,559
nursery school	533	3,284	4,212
public	403	1,314	1,868
private	130	1,969	2,344
kindergarten	602	3,163	4,034
public	539	2,596	3,353
private	63	567	680
elementary school	4,427	24,667	31,467
public	4,146	21,763	28,116
private	281	2,905	3,351
high school	1,935	11,857	15,049
public	1,839	10,809	13,865
private	96	1,048	1,184

SOURCE: U.S. Bureau of the Census, <u>Current Population Reports: School Enrollment-Social and Economic Characteristics of Students:</u> <u>October 1988 and 1987</u>, Series P-20, #443, pp. 166-167, table A2; <u>October 1991</u>, Series P-20, #469, pp. A2-A5, Table A-1; <u>October 1996(Update)</u>, Series P-20, #500, pp. 21-22, Table 5. C3.186/12:(year)

NOTES: 'Total' includes other races and ethnic groups not shown separately.

UNITS: Enrollment in thousands of persons enrolled; civilian non-institutionalized population.

Table 4.03 Estimates of the School Age Population, by Age and Sex, 1996

	Hispanic	White	Total
Both sexes			
3-34 years old	17,050	99,199	124,447
3 and 4 years old	1,318	6,374	8,193
5 and 6 years old	1,328	6,558	8,393
7-9 years old	1,643	9,309	11,905
10-13 years old	2,173	12,359	15,661
14 and 15 years old	1,013	6,120	7,750
16 and 17 years old	971	6,118	7,782
18 and 19 years old	1,000	5,833	7,376
20 and 21 years old	965	5,410	6,800
22-24 years old	1,545	8,433	10,495
25-29 years old	2,524	15,436	18,982
30-34 years old	2,570	17,249	21,111
35 years old and over	9,823	110,308	128,729
Male			
3-34 years old	8,771	50,238	62,510
3 and 4 years old	637	3,268	4,182
5 and 6 years old	681	3,362	4,320
7-9 years old	823	4,775	6,098
10-13 years old	1,109	6,339	7,957
14 and 15 years old	522	3,139	3,989
16 and 17 years old	498	3,146	4,012
18 and 19 years old	506	2,953	3,711
20 and 21 years old	486	2,638	3,268
22-24 years old	823	4,306	5,306
25-29 years old	1,306	7,691	9,295
30-34 years old	1,379	8,620	10,372
35 years old and over	4,692	52,387	60,593

continued on the next page

Table 4.03   continued

	Hispanic	White	Total
Female			
3-34 years old	8,280	48,961	61,937
3 and 4 years old	681	3,105	4,011
5 and 6 years old	647	3,196	4,073
7-9 years old	820	4,534	5,807
10-13 years old	1,064	6,020	7,704
14 and 15 years old	491	2,981	3,761
16 and 17 years old	474	2,972	3,769
18 and 19 years old	494	2,879	3,665
20 and 21 years old	479	2,772	3,532
22-24 years old	721	4,127	5,189
25-29 years old	1,218	7,745	9,687
30-34 years old	1,191	8,629	10,738
35 years old and over	5,131	57,921	68,136

SOURCE: U.S. Bureau of the Census, <u>Current Population Reports: School Enrollment-Social and Economic Characteristics of Students:</u> <u>October 1996 (Update)</u>, Series P-20, #500, pp. 1-3, table 1. <www.census.gov/prod/3/98pubs/p20-500u.pdf>,, accessed 15 October 1998.

NOTES: 'Total' includes other races and ethnic groups not shown separately.

UNITS: Estimates of the civilian non-institutionalized population, 3-34 years old as of October 1, in thousands of persons.

Table 4.04 Preprimary School Enrollment of Children 3 - 6 Years Old, by Selected Characteristic of the Mother, 1996

	Hispanic	White	Total
1996			
All children 3 and 4 years old enrolled in nursery school	433	2,847	3,655
with mother in labor force	227	1,828	2,385
- mother employed	211	1,745	2,236
- employed full time	146	1,091	1,465
with mother with 0-8 years of school	80	95	99
with mother high school graduate	100	734	956
with mother with bachelor's degree	44	856	1,031
All children 3 and 4 years old enrolled in kindergarten	70	205	304
with mother in labor force	24	106	170
- mother employed	22	102	151
- employed full time	17	67	108
with mother with 0-8 years of school	20	24	24
with mother high school graduate	11	49	75
with mother with bachelor's degree	5	34	39

continued on the next page

Table 4.04   continued

	Hispanic	White	Total
All children 5 years old enrolled in nursery school	95	382	492
with mother in labor force	37	225	303
- mother employed	31	212	275
- employed full time	26	149	199
with mother with 0-8 years of school	24	26	33
with mother high school graduate	28	117	150
with mother with bachelor's degree	-	78	90
All children 5 years old enrolled in kindergarten	471	2,469	3,129
with mother in labor force	258	1,526	1,964
- mother employed	238	1,451	1,835
- employed full time	200	937	1,245
with mother with 0-8 years of school	109	127	142
with mother high school graduate	98	710	889
with mother with bachelor's degree	24	525	612

SOURCE: U.S. Bureau of the Census, Current Population Reports: School Enrollment-Social and Economic Characteristics of Students: October 1996(Update), Series P-20, #500, pp. 15-18, table 4. C3 <www.census.gov/prod/3/98pubs/p20-500u.pdf>, accessed 15 October 1998.

NOTES: 'Total' includes other races/ethnic groups not shown separately. Includes children enrolled in public and non-public nursery school and kindergarten programs. Excludes five year olds enrolled in elementary school. 'All children' includes children whose mothers' labor force status is unknown and children with no mother present in the household.

UNITS: Enrollment in thousands of children enrolled.

Hispanic Americans: A Statistical Sourcebook

Table 4.05 Enrollment in Public Elementary and Secondary Schools, by State, Fall, 1996

	Hispanic	White	Total
Alabama	0.7%	61.5%	100.0%
Alaska	2.9	63.1	"
Arizona	30.1	56.6	"
Arkansas	1.8	73.5	"
California	39.7	39.5	"
Colorado	18.8	72.0	"
Connecticut	11.9	71.7	"
Delaware	4.3	63.9	"
District of Columbia	7.2	4.0	"
Florida	15.9	56.7	"
Georgia	2.6	57.9	"
Hawaii	4.9	25.0	"
Idaho	8.9	88.0	"
Illinois	12.8	62.8	"
Indiana	2.4	85.4	"
Iowa	2.4	92.2	"
Kansas	6.5	81.9	"
Kentucky	0.5	88.9	"
Louisiana	1.2	50.6	"
Maine	0.4	97.2	"
Maryland	3.5	56.7	"
Massachusetts	9.6	77.9	"
Michigan	2.8	75.8	"
Minnesota	2.2	86.5	"
Mississippi	0.4	47.9	"
Missouri	1.1	81.1	"
Montana	1.5	87.2	"
Nebraska	4.9	86.4	"
Nevada	18.8	65.1	"
New Hampshire	1.3	96.4	"
New Jersey	na	na	"

continued on the next page

Table 4.05   continued

	Hispanic	White	Total
New Mexico	47.7%	38.8%	100.0%
New York	17.6	56.3	"
North Carolina	2.3	63.9	"
North Dakota	1.1	89.1	"
Ohio	1.4	82.0	"
Oklahoma	4.3	68.8	"
Oregon	7.4	84.6	"
Pennsylvania	3.7	80.2	"
Rhode Island	10.7	78.3	"
South Carolina	0.8	56.0	"
South Dakota	0.8	83.7	"
Tennessee	0.9	74.6	"
Texas	37.4	45.6	"
Utah	6.0	89.5	"
Vermont	0.4	97.3	"
Virginia	3.3	67.7	"
Washington	8.3	77.5	"
West Virginia	0.5	95.2	"
Wisconsin	3.5	82.6	"
Wyoming	6.2	89.0	"

SOURCE: U.S. Department of Education, Center for Education Statistics, <u>Digest of Education Statistics, 1998</u>, p. 11, table 45. ED 1.113\998

NOTES: 'Total' includes other races and ethnic groups not shown separately. 'White' excludes persons of Hispanic origin.

UNITS: Enrollment as a percent of total enrollment, 100.0%.

Table 4.06 Public Elementary and Secondary School Teachers, by Selected Characteristic, 1993-94

	Hispanic	White	Total
Total number of teachers	108,744	2,216,605	2,561,294
Percent of teachers, by highest degree earned			
no degree	0.9%	0.5%	0.6%
associate degree	0.5	0.1	0.2
bachelor's degree	62.8	51.8	52.0
master's degree	29.8	42.5	42.0
education specialist	4.6	4.4	4.6
doctor's	1.4	0.7	0.7
Percent of teachers, by years of full-time teaching experience			
less than 3 years	16.7%	9.4%	9.7%
3-9 years	32.1	25.5	25.5
10-20 years	34.1	35.2	35.0
over 20 years	17.1	30.0	29.8

SOURCE: U.S. Department of Education, Center for Education Statistics, <u>Digest of Education Statistics, 1995</u>, p. 77, table 66 (data from U.S. Department of Educations, National Center for Education Statististics, *Schools and Staffing Survey, 1993-94*). ED 1.113\995

NOTES: 'Total' includes other races and ethnic groups not shown separately. 'White' excludes persons of Hispanic origin.

UNITS: Percent, as a percent of all public elementary and secondary school teachers, 100.0%.

Table 4.07 Private Elementary and Secondary School Teachers, by Selected
Characteristic, 1993-94

	Hispanic	White	Total
Total number of teachers	12,221	347,811	378,365
Percent of teachers, by highest degree earned			
no degree	11.1%	4.8%	5.2%
associate degree	4.9	1.3	1.5
bachelor's degree	57.4	59.4	59.0
master's degree	19.9	30.2	29.8
education specialist	4.4	2.6	2.9
doctor's	2.3	1.6	1.7
Percent of teachers, by years of full-time teaching experience			
less than 3 years	25.5%	20.4%	20.9%
3-9 years	41.8	33.6	33.9
10-20 years	21.6	30.0	29.6
over 20 years	11.1	16.0	15.6

SOURCE: U.S. Department of Education, Center for Education Statistics, <u>Digest of Education Statistics, 1995</u>, p. 77, table 66 (data from U.S. Department of Educations, National Center for Education Statistics, *Schools and Staffing Survey, 1993-95*). ED 1.113\995

NOTES: 'Total' includes other races and ethnic groups not shown separately. 'White' excludes persons of Hispanic origin.

UNITS: Percent, as a percent of all private elementary and secondary school teachers, 100.0%.

Table 4.08 Student Achievement: Reading and Writing Performance on
Standardized Tests, 1984, 1990 and 1996

	Hispanic	White	Total
Reading			
1984			
students age 9	187.2	218.2	210.9
students age 13	239.6	262.6	257.1
students age 17	268.1	295.2	288.8
1990			
students age 9	189.4	217.0	209.2
students age 13	237.8	262.3	256.8
students age 17	274.8	296.6	290.2
1996			
students age 9	194.1	219.9	212.4
students age 13	239.9	267.0	259.1
students age 17	264.7	294.4	286.9
Writing			
1984			
students grade 4	188.5	210.7	203.8
students grade 8	246.9	271.7	266.7
students grade 11	259.1	296.8	289.7
1990			
students grade 4	184.1	211.0	201.7
students grade 8	245.7	262.1	256.6
students grade 11	276.9	292.8	287.1
1996			
students grade 4	191	216	207
students grade 8	246	271	264
students grade 11	269	289	283

SOURCE: U.S. Department of Education, Center for Education Statistics, <u>Digest
of Education Statistics, 1997</u>, table 107, p. 114; table 113, p. 120.
ED 1.113:997

NOTES: 'Total' includes other races and ethnic groups not shown separately.

UNITS: Reading level shown as scale score on scale: 150=rudimentary,
200=basic, 250=intermediate, 300=adept, 350=advanced.
Writing level shown as score on scale: 100=unsatisfactory,
200=minimal, 300=adequate, 400=elaborate.

Table 4.09 Student Achievement: Math and Science Proficiency, 1986, 1990 and 1996

	Hispanic	White	Total
Average mathematics proficiency			
1986			
students age 9	205.4	226.9	221.7
students age 13	254.3	273.6	269.0
students age 17	283.1	307.5	302.0
1990			
students age 9	213.8	235.2	229.6
students age 13	254.6	276.3	270.4
students age 17	283.5	309.5	304.6
1996			
students age 9	215	237	231
students age 13	256	281	274
students age 17	292	313	307
Average science proficiency			
1986			
students age 9	199.4·	231.9	224.3
students age 13	226.1	259.2	251.4
students age 17	259.3	297.5	288.5
1990			
students age 9	206.2	237.5	228.7
students age 13	231.6	264.1	255.2
students age 17	261.5	300.9	290.4
1996			
students age 9	207	239	230
students age 13	232	266	256
students age 17	269	307	296

SOURCE: U.S. Department of Education, Center for Education Statistics, <u>Digest of Education Statistics, 1997</u>, table 118, p. 123; table 126, p. 131. ED 1.113:994

NOTES: 'Total' includes other races and ethnic groups not shown separately.

UNITS: Math proficiency scale: 150=performs simple addition and subtraction, 200= use basic operations to solve simple problems, 250=uses intermediate level mathematics skills to solve two-step problems, 300=understands measurement and geometry and solves more complex problems, 350= understands and applies more advanced mathematical concepts.

Table 4.10 Expected Occupations of 12th Graders at Age 30, 1992

	Hispanic	White	Total
Expected occupation at age 30			
craftsperson or operator	2.7%	3.7%	3.5%
farmer or farm manager	0.7	1.0	0.9
housewife/homemaker	0.7	1.2	1.0
laborer or farm worker	0.6	0.7	0.7
military, police or security officer	7.4	6.4	6.6
professional, business or			
managerial	47.1	50.0	50.8
teacher	6.7	8.4	7.5
business owner	7.7	5.6	6.0
technical	7.5	5.0	5.4
salesperson, clerical or office			
worker	6.4	4.6	4.8
service worker	2.5	2.3	2.4
other employment	9.6	10.8	10.2
don't know	0.5	0.2	0.2

SOURCE: U.S. Department of Education, Center for Education Statistics, Digest of Education Statistics, 1994, p. 136, table 140 (data from the National Educational Longitudinal Study 1988, Second Followup). ED 1.113:992

NOTES: 'Total' includes other races and ethnic groups not shown separately.

UNITS: Percent of 10th graders as a percent of all 10th graders, by race.

Table 4.11 Labor Force Status of 1997 High School Graduates and 1996-97 High School Dropouts, October 1997

	Hispanic	White	Total
1997 high school graduates			
total	188	1,337	1,590
employed	141	1,168	1,362
unemployed	47	169	228
not in labor force	148	891	1,179
1996-97 high school dropouts			
total	88	250	302
employed	73	199	225
unemployed	15	51	77
not in labor force	32	136	200

SOURCE: U.S. Department Labor, Bureau Labor Statistics; "Employment Characteristics of Families, 1997 (Table) 1. Labor force status of 1997 high school graduates and 1996-97 high school dropouts 16 to 24 years old by school enrollment, sex, race, and Hispanic origin"; (accessed: 19 November 1998); < http://stats.bls.gov/news.release/hsgec.t0l.htm >

NOTES: 'High school dropouts' refers to persons who dopped out of school between October 1995 and October 1996.

UNITS: Number of persons in thousands of persons.

Table 4.12 High School Dropout Rates, Grades 10-12, by Sex, 1975 - 1994

	Hispanic		White		Total	
	male	female	male	female	male	female
1975	10.1%	11.6%	5.0%	5.8%	5.4%	6.2%
1980	16.9	6.9	6.4	4.9	6.6	5.4
1981	10.6	10.9	5.6	4.9	6.0	5.8
1982	9.5	9.0	5.3	4.9	5.7	5.1
1983	13.7	6.2	5.4	4.2	5.7	4.6
1984	12.2	10.1	5.3	4.6	5.4	4.7
1985	9.3	9.8	3.0	4.5	5.4	5.0
1986	11.7	12.4	4.2	4.1	4.3	4.2
1987	5.0	6.2	4.1	3.4	4.4	3.8
1988	12.3	8.4	5.1	4.3	5.2	4.5
1989	7.6	7.7	4.1	3.8	4.5	4.5
1990	8.7	7.2	4.1	3.5	4.1	3.9
1991	10.4	4.8	3.6	3.8	3.8	4.3
1992	5.8	8.6	3.8	4.4	3.8	4.8
1993	5.1	7.5	4.1	4.1	4.4	4.1
1994	8.4	10.1	4.6	4.9	4.9	5.1

SOURCE: U.S. Bureau of the Census, Current Population Reports: School Enrollment-Social and Economic Characteristics of Students: October 1994, Series P-20, #487, pp. A25-28, table A-4. C3.186/12:994

NOTES: 'Total' includes other races and ethnic groups not shown separately.

UNITS: Percent, as a percent of all persons 16-24 years of age.

Chapter 5: Education - Postsecondary & Educational Attainment

Table 5.01 Enrollment in Institutions of Higher Education, by Type of Institution, 1980 - 1995

	Hispanic	White	Total
1980			
All institutions	1,107	9,883	12,087
4-year institutions	634	6,275	7,565
2-year institutions	472	3,558	4,521
1986			
All institutions	1,081	9,915	12,501
4-year institutions	615	6,340	7,826
2-year institutions	466	3,575	4,675
1988			
All institutions	1,130	10,283	13,043
4-year institutions	656	6,582	8,175
2-year institutions	473	3,702	4,868
1990			
All institutions	1,223	10,675	13,710
4-year institutions	715	6,757	8,529
2-year institutions	509	3,918	5,181
1992			
All institutions	955.0	10,875.4	14,487.4
4-year institutions	410.0	6,744.3	8,765.0
2-year institutions	545.0	4,131.2	5,722.4
1995 (preliminary)			
All institutions	1,473.7	10,311.2	14,261.8
4-year institutions	852.2	6,517.2	8,769.3
2-year institutions	621.5	3,794.0	5,492.5

SOURCE: U.S. Department of Education, Center for Education Statistics, Condition of Education, 1993, p. 345, table 44-1. ED 1.109:993
U.S. Department of Education, Center for Education Statistics, Digest of Education Statistics, 1997, p. 214, table 206. ED 1.113:996

NOTES: 'Total' includes other races and ethnic groups not shown separately. 'White' excludes persons of Hispanic origin.

UNITS: Enrollment in thousands of students enrolled.

Table 5.02 Enrollment in Institutions of Higher Education, by State, Fall, 1996

	Hispanic	White	Total
UNITED STATES	1,152,229	10,226,034	14,300,255
Alabama	1,739	157,161	219,499
Alaska	713	22,369	28,846
Arizona	40,063	200,429	276,832
Arkansas	835	80,089	100,688
California	383,461	922,781	1,882,634
Colorado	23,226	193,944	242,949
Connecticut	8,020	123,344	155,361
Delaware	901	35,287	44,838
District of Columbia	2,978	35,897	74,239
Florida	92,087	418,043	641,173
Georgia	4,987	214,549	317,999
Hawaii	1,342	16,394	61,383
Idaho	1,695	54,827	59,904
Illinois	63,923	504,144	720,987
Indiana	6,571	246,370	286,326
Iowa	2,906	156,705	177,021
Kansas	6,233	145,757	172,350
Kentucky	1,196	158,077	177,749
Louisiana	5,014	133,455	203,517
Maine	376	52,887	55,645
Maryland	6,350	170,259	260,757
Massachusetts	17,788	316,804	410,327
Michigan	11,694	436,671	546,974
Minnesota	3,756	243,962	275,262
Mississippi	698	83,659	126,234
Missouri	4,995	243,600	290,533
Montana	504	37,389	43,145
Nebraska	2,393	107,274	119,300
Nevada	6,236	55,008	73,467
New Hampshire	864	60,068	64,463

continued on the next page

Table 5.02   continued

	Hispanic	White	Total
New Jersey	31,982	223,256	328,188
New Mexico	33,232	57,323	103,546
New York	102,835	672,311	1,027,870
North Carolina	4,965	275,630	373,168
North Dakota	286	35,916	40,554
Ohio	8,163	448,218	537,535
Oklahoma	4,280	133,516	177,255
Oregon	5,764	138,104	165,168
Pennsylvania	11,734	518,526	621,994
Rhode Island	2,970	60,722	72,432
South Carolina	1,639	126,593	174,303
South Dakota	175	31,431	35,373
Tennessee	2,595	198,139	247,043
Texas	202,451	582,317	955,439
Utah	4,130	136,543	151,637
Vermont	490	32,762	35,090
Virginia	8,447	260,077	353,788
Washington	11,410	231,505	292,180
West Virginia	517	78,727	85,689
Wisconsin	6,307	264,203	299,127
Wyoming	1,384	27,976	30,805

SOURCE: U.S. Department of Education, Center for Education Statistics, <u>Digest of Education Statistics, 1998</u>, p. 259, table 210. ED 1.113\998

NOTES: 'Total' includes other races and ethnic groups not shown separately. 'White' excludes Hispanic.

UNITS: Enrollment in number of students enrolled.

Table 5.03 Enrollment Rates of 18 - 24 Year Olds in Institutions of Higher Education, 1975 - 1996

	Hispanic	White	Total
Enrollment as a percent of 18-24 year olds			
1975	20.4%	27.4%	26.3%
1980	19.4	27.3	25.7
1981	19.9	27.7	26.2
1983	19.2	28.0	26.2
1984	20.3	28.9	27.1
1986	21.9	29.7	27.9
1987	23.0	31.9	29.7
1988	21.1	33.1	30.2
1990	25.3	35.2	32.1
1991	23.4	36.8	33.3
1992	25.2	37.3	34.4
1993	24.5	36.8	34.0
1994	18.8	38.1	34.6
1995	20.7	37.9	34.3
1996	20.1	39.5	35.5
Enrollment as a percent of high school graduates			
1975	31.5%	32.3%	32.5%
1980	27.6	32.1	31.8
1981	28.0	32.7	32.5
1983	27.0	33.0	32.5
1984	27.2	34.0	33.2
1986	28.6	34.5	34.0
1987	30.0	37.5	36.4
1988	28.0	38.6	37.2
1990	30.4	39.2	37.7
1991	28.2	41.0	39.3
1992	33.9	42.8	42.0
1993	32.8	42.6	41.6
1994	33.1	43.7	42.3
1995	35.2	44.0	42.3
1996	34.5	45.1	43.4

Source: U.S. Department of Education, Center for Education Statistics, <u>Digest of Education Statistics, 1997</u> p. 196, table 186. ED 1.113\997

NOTES: 'Total' includes other races and ethnic groups not shown separately. 'White' does not include Hispanic.

UNITS: Percent as a percent of 18-24 year olds, and high school graduates as shown, 100.0%.

Table 5.04 Enrollment of Persons 14 - 34 Years Old in Institutions of Higher Education, by Sex, 1975 - 1996

	enrollment			percent distribution		
	Hispanic	White	Total	Hispanic	White	Total
1975						
Total	927	8,141	9,697	9.6%	84.0%	100.0%
men	433	4,566	5,342	4.5	47.1	55.1
women	494	3,576	4,355	5.1	36.9	44.9
1980						
Total	996	8,453	10,181	9.8%	83.0%	100.0%
men	431	4,225	5,193	4.2	41.5	51.0
women	565	4,228	5,244	5.5	41.5	49.0
1985						
Total	1,036	8,781	10,863	9.5%	80.0%	100.0%
men	458	4,361	5,345	4.2	40.1	49.2
women	578	4,420	5,518	5.3	40.7	50.8
1990						
Total	1,167	8,892	11,303	10.3%	78.7%	100.0%
men	508	4,289	na	4.5	38.0	na
women	659	4,594	na	5.8	40.6	na
1993						
Total	1,227	8,592	11,409	10.8%	75.3%	100.0%
men	515	4,168	na	4.5	36.5	na
women	713	4,424	na	6.2	38.8	na
1996						
Total	1,039	8,943	12,448	8.3%	71.8%	100.0%
men	440	4,222	na	3.5	33.9	na
women	599	4,721	na	4.8	37.9	na

SOURCE: U.S. Department of Education, Center for Education Statistics, <u>Digest of Education Statistics, 1997</u>, p. 221, table 212. ED 1.113\997

NOTES: 'Total' includes other races and ethnic groups not shown separately. 'White' excludes Hispanic.

UNITS: Enrollment in thousands of students enrolled; percent as a percentage of 14-34 year olds, by sex as shown, 100.0%.

Table 5.05 Enrollment in Institutions of Higher Education, by Control of the Institution, Fall, 1980 - 1996

	Hispanic	White	Total
1980			
both public and private control	460	9,033	10,473
public control	364	6,677	7,781
private control	96	2,356	2,692
1986			
both public and private control	706	9,098	10,784
public control	568	6,951	8,312
private control	138	2,148	2,472
1988			
both public and private control	654	9,244	10,937
public control	592	7,302	8,663
private control	62	1,940	2,278
1990			
both public and private control	617	9,465	11,303
public control	518	7,410	8,887
private control	100	2,055	2,416
1991			
both public and private control	721	9,579	11,589
public control	607	7,464	9,078
private control	115	2,118	2,511
1996			
both public and private control	1,223	12,189	15,226
public control	1,031	9,566	12,014
private control	192	2,622	3,212

SOURCE: U.S. Bureau of the Census, Current Population Reports: School Enrollment-Social and Economic Characteristics of Students: October 1994, Series P-20, #487, pp. A2-A4, Table A-1; 1996(Update), #500, pp. 33-36, Table 9. C3.186/12:(year)

NOTES: 'Total' includes other races and ethnic groups not shown separately. 'White' excludes Hispanic persons.

UNITS: Enrollment in thousands of students.

Table 5.06 College Enrollment This Year, by Enrollment Status Last Year, by Age, October 1996

	Hispanic	White	Total
All persons 15 years old and over			
Not enrolled in college in 1996			
total	9,146	123,402	144,450
not enrolled in 1994	8,765	118,462	138,469
enrolled in 1994	381	4,941	5,981
Enrolled in college in 1996			
total	1,187	12,109	15,098
not enrolled in 1994	260	2,540	3,212
enrolled in 1994	927	9,569	11,886
enrolled full time in 1996			
total	689	7,805	9,761
not enrolled in 1994	100	1,000	1,302
enrolled in 1994	589	6,805	8,459
Persons 15-19 years old			
Not enrolled in college in 1996			
total	241	1,523	1,994
not enrolled in 1994	153	784	1,020
enrolled in 1994	87	739	974
Enrolled in college in 1996			
total	248	2,855	3,483
not enrolled in 1994	40	272	332
enrolled in 1994	209	2,583	3,151
enrolled full time in 1996			
total	190	2,551	3,101
not enrolled in 1994	28	204	248
enrolled in 1994	162	2,347	2,853

continued on the next page

Table 5.06   continued

	Hispanic	White	Total
Persons 20-24 years old			
Not enrolled in college in 1996			
total	1,078	7,623	9,467
not enrolled in 1994	965	6,234	7,798
enrolled in 1994	112	1,389	1,669
Enrolled in college in 1996			
total	456	4,384	5,440
not enrolled in 1994	84	664	850
enrolled in 1994	372	3,719	4,591
enrolled full time in 1996			
total	328	3,571	4,433
not enrolled in 1994	45	405	539
enrolled in 1994	283	3,166	3,894
Persons 25 years old and over			
Not enrolled in college in 1996			
total	7,828	114,257	132,990
not enrolled in 1994	7,646	111,444	129,652
enrolled in 1994	181	2,813	3,338
Enrolled in college in 1996			
total	483	4,870	6,174
not enrolled in 1994	137	1,603	2,030
enrolled in 1994	346	3,267	4,144
enrolled full time in 1996			
total	171	1,683	2,227
not enrolled in 1994	27	391	515
enrolled in 1994	144	1,292	1,712

SOURCE: U.S. Bureau of the Census, Current Population Reports: School Enrollment-Social and Economic Characteristics of Students: October 1996 (Update), Series P-20, #500u, pp. 73-77, table 18. <www.census.gov/prod/3/98pubs/p20-500u.pdf>, accessed 15 October 1998.

NOTES: 'Total' includes other races and ethnic groups not shown separately. College in enrollment at the undergraduate level in two and four year institutions.

UNITS: College enrollment in thousands of students. Institutions of Higher Education, by Sex, 1975 - 1990

Table 5.07   Undergraduates Receiving Financial Aid: Average Amount
Awarded per Student, by Type and Source of Aid, 1995-96

	Hispanic	White	Total
1995-96			
All full-time, full-year	588	4,500	6,306
enrolled undergraduates			
undergraduates receiving:			
any aid			
total	$ 5,999	$ 6,836	$ 6,832
- from federal source	4,644	5,549	5,362
- from non-federal sources	3,328	3,848	3,883
grants			
total	$ 3,486	$ 3,762	$ 3,864
- from federal source	2,113	1,894	2,001
- from non-federal sources	3,017	3,541	3,599
loans			
total	$ 4,168	$ 4,437	$ 4,345
- from federal source	4,137	4,366	4,288
- from non-federal sources	2,235	2,912	2,747
work-study funds			
total	$ 1,152	$ 1,367	$ 1,371

SOURCE: U.S. Department of Education, Center for Education Statistics, <u>Digest</u>
<u>of Education Statistics, 1997</u>, p. 330, table 315. ED 1.113\997

NOTES: 'Total' includes other races and ethnic groups not shown separately.
'White' excludes Hispanic persons.

UNITS: Average 1992-93 award in dollars per student, for students enrolled in
Fall, 1992. Number of undergraduates, in thousands.

Table 5.08   Employment Status of Students 16 - 24 Years of Age, Enrolled in School, 1996

	Hispanic	White	Total
All students 16-24 years of age enrolled in school in the civilian labor force	1,644	11,708	14,904
number	653	6,164	7,286
percent	39.7%	52.6%	48.9%
employed	531	5,546	6,448
unemployed	122	618	838
All high school students 16-24 years of age enrolled in school in the civilian labor force	1,034	5,960	7,687
number	284	2,628	3,087
percent	27.4%	44.1%	40.2%
employed	206	2,234	2,559
unemployed	78	394	528
All college students 16-24 years of age enrolled in school in the civilian labor force	609	5,748	7,217
number	369	3,536	4,199
percent	60.5%	61.5%	58.2%
employed	325	3,312	3,889
unemployed	44	224	310

SOURCE: U.S. Department of Labor, Bureau of Labor Statistics, *Employment and Earnings*, January, 1997, p. 166, table 7, (data from the Current Population Survey). L 2.41/2:37/1:997

NOTES: 'Total' includes other races and ethnic groups not shown separately.

UNITS: Number of students in thousands; percent as a percent of the civilian noninstitutional population 16-24 years of age.

Table 5.09 Enrollment in Schools of Medicine, Dentistry and Related Fields, 1980-81 and 1995-96

	Hispanic	White	Total
1980-81			
allopathic medicine	4.2%	85.0%	100.0%
osteopathic medicine	1.1	94.9	"
podiatry	1.5	91.3	"
dentistry	2.3	88.5	"
optometry	1.8	91.4	"
pharmacy	2.1	88.6	"
veterinary medicine	1.1	95.2	"
registered nursing	na	na	
1995-96			
allopathic medicine	6.5%	66.6%	100.0%
osteopathic medicine	3.9	80.3	"
podiatry	4.3	77.2	"
dentistry	4.8	68.0	"
optometry	3.8	75.4	"
pharmacy	2.8	71.9	"
registered nursing	3.5	82.4	"

SOURCE: U.S. Department of Health and Human Services, Health United States, 1992, p. 150, table 105; 1998, pp. 331-332, table 107 (data from the Association of American Medical Colleges, American Association of Colleges of Osteopathic Medicine, National League for Nursing, American Association of Colleges of Podiatric Medicine, American Dental Association American Optometric Association, American Association of Colleges of Pharmacy, Association of American Veterinary Medical Colleges). HE 20.6223:(year)

NOTES: 'Total' includes other races and ethnic groups not shown separately. 'White' excludes Hispanic persons.

UNITS: Enrollment as a percentage of all students enrolled, 100.0%.

Table 5.10 Earned Degrees Conferred, by Type of Degree, 1979 - 1996

	Hispanic	White	Total
1979			
Bachelor's degrees	60,130	799,617	916,347
Master's degrees	19,393	249,051	299,887
Doctor's degrees	1,267	26,128	32,664
First Professional degrees	2,836	62,430	68,611
1981			
Bachelor's degrees	60,673	807,319	934,800
Master's degrees	17,133	241,216	294,183
Doctor's degrees	1,265	25,908	32,839
First Professional degrees	2,931	64,551	71,340
1985			
Bachelor's degrees	57,473	826,106	968,311
Master's degrees	13,939	223,628	280,421
Doctor's degrees	1,154	23,934	32,307
First Professional degrees	3,029	63,219	71,057
1991-92			
Bachelor's degrees	40,761	936,771	1,129,833
Master's degrees	9,358	268,371	348,682
Doctor's degrees	811	25,813	40,090
First Professional degrees	2,766	59,800	72,129
1995-96			
Bachelor's degrees	58,288	904,709	1,163,036
Master's degrees	14,412	297,558	405,521
Doctor's degrees	999	27,756	44,645
First Professional degrees	3,476	59,456	76,641

SOURCE: U.S. Department of Education, Center for Education Statistics, 1989 Education Indicators, pp. 228-229, table 2:5-1. ED 1.109:989
U.S. Department of Education, Center for Education Statistics, Digest of Education Statistics, 1994, pp. 276-288, tables 252-264; 1998, p. 337, table 266, p. 340, table 269, p. 343, table 272, p. 346, table 275. ED 1.113\9(year)

NOTES: 'Total' includes other races and ethnic groups not shown separately. 'White' excludes Hispanic persons. 'First professional Degrees' include degrees awarded in chiropractic, dentistry, law, medicine, optometry, osteopathy, pharmacy, podiatry, theology, and veterinary medicine.

UNITS: Earned degrees conferred in number of degrees.

Table 5.11 Associate Degrees Conferred, by Major Field of Study, 1994-95

	Hispanic	White	Total
All Fields, Total	36,013	419,323	538,545
agriculture and natural resources	118	5,380	5,730
architecture and related programs	17	243	277
area, ethnic and cultural studies	8	19	68
biological sciences/life sciences	191	1,225	1,879
business and management	6,972	76,068	101,926
communications	135	2,687	3,160
communications technologies	155	1,512	1,984
computer and information sciences	757	6,470	9,152
construction trades	68	1,456	1,728
education	855	7,350	9,658
engineering	121	1,703	2,232
engineering technologies	2,405	27,453	34,732
English language and literature/letters	194	756	1,548
foreign languages and literatures	78	466	616
health professions and related sciences	3,654	83,473	98,474
home economics	667	5,580	7,821
law and legal studies	637	7,278	9,140
liberal/general studies	12,574	130,736	170,817
library science	0	91	101
mathematics	101	488	782
mechanics and repairers	755	9,089	11,497
multi/interdisciplinary studies	434	6,863	8,692
parks, recreation, and fitness studies	50	680	864
philosophy and religion	9	66	81
physical sciences	132	1,840	2,456
precision production trades	734	7,605	9,344
protective services	2,078	15,395	19,709
psychology	196	1,163	1,600
public administration and services	360	2,484	3,882
military technologies	28	279	364
social sciences and history	361	2,418	3,634
theological studies/religious vocations	21	521	607
transportation	103	1,154	1,446
visual and performing arts	1,045	9,332	12,544

SOURCE: U.S. Department of Education, Center for Education Statistics, <u>Digest of Education Statistics, 1997</u>, p. 293, table 263. ED 1.113\997

NOTES: 'Total' includes other races and ethnic groups not shown separately. 'White' excludes Hispanic persons.

UNITS: Earned Associate degrees conferred in number of degrees.

Table 5.12   Bachelor's Degrees Conferred, by Major Field of Study, 1995-96

	Hispanic	White	Total
All Fields, Total	58,288	904,709	1,163,036
agriculture and natural resources	573	19,286	21,431
architecture and related programs	576	6,293	8,352
area, ethnic and cultural studies	573	3,583	5,786
biological sciences/life sciences	2,616	44,676	60,994
business and management	11,286	168,220	227,102
communications	2,049	38,144	47,320
communications technologies	9	564	683
computer and information sciences	1,042	15,827	24,098
construction trades	0	73	80
education	3,792	91,259	105,509
engineering	2,883	44,185	62,114
engineering technologies	748	11,719	15,189
English language and literature/letters	2,235	42,166	50,698
foreign languages and literatures	2,122	10,137	13,952
health professions and related sciences	2,912	69,156	84,036
home economics	448	13,351	15,803
law and legal studies	104	1,634	2,052
liberal/general studies	2,470	26,053	33,997
library science	0	52	58
mathematics	558	10,033	13,143
mechanics and repairers	2	39	54
multi/interdisciplinary studies	2,192	20,043	26,515
parks, recreation, and fitness studies	579	12,146	13,983
philosophy and religion	307	6,182	7,388
physical sciences	566	15,551	19,647
precision production trades	13	345	401
protective services	1,918	18,386	24,810
psychology	4,640	57,254	73,291
public administration and services	1,290	14,205	19,849
military technologies	0	7	7
social sciences and history	7,366	96,637	126,479
theological studies/religious vocations	106	4,740	5,358
transportation	137	3,020	3,561
visual and performing arts	2,176	39,743	49,296

SOURCE: U.S. Department of Education, Center for Education Statistics, Digest of Education Statistics, 1998, p. 337, table 266. ED 1.113\998

NOTES: 'Total' includes other races and ethnic groups not shown separately. 'White' excludes Hispanic persons.

UNITS: Earned Bachelor's degrees conferred in number of degrees.

Table 5.13 Master's Degrees Conferred, by Major Field of Study, 1995-96

	Hispanic	White	Total
All Fields, Total	14,412	297,558	405,521
agriculture and natural resources	101	3,334	4,569
architecture and related programs	187	2,664	3,993
area, ethnic and cultural studies	99	1,198	1,713
biological sciences/life sciences	161	4,262	6,157
business and management	2,938	65,685	93,982
communications	146	3,471	5,080
communications technologies	15	297	524
computer and information sciences	178	4,382	10,151
construction trades	0	0	0
education	4,628	87,310	106,253
engineering	707	14,250	27,441
engineering technologies	36	843	1,125
English language and literature/letters	228	6,736	7,893
foreign languages and literatures	322	2,054	3,124
health professions and related sciences	996	27,008	33,398
home economics	94	2,293	2,917
law and legal studies	79	1,245	2,751
liberal/general studies	70	2,347	2,778
library science	116	4,411	5,099
mathematics	92	2,430	4,031
multi/interdisciplinary studies	73	1,865	2,347
parks, recreation, and fitness studies	36	1,483	1,751
philosophy and religion	39	1,067	1,302
physical sciences	102	3,548	5,847
precision production trades	0	6	8
protective services	64	1,437	1,812
psychology	682	11,249	13,792
public administration and services	1,267	17,968	24,229
military technologies	0	127	136
social sciences and history	511	10,339	15,012
theological studies/religious vocations	95	3,858	5,107
transportation	26	830	919
visual and performing arts	324	7,561	10,280

SOURCE: U.S. Department of Education, Center for Education Statistics, <u>Digest of Education Statistics, 1998</u>, p. 340, table 269. ED 1.113\998

NOTES: 'Total' includes other races and ethnic groups not shown separately. 'White' excludes Hispanic persons.

UNITS: Earned Master's degrees conferred in number of degrees.

Table 5.14 Doctor's Degrees Conferred, by Major Field of Study, 1995-96

	Hispanic	White	Total
All Fields, Total	999	27,756	44,645
agriculture and natural resources	11	575	1,271
architecture and related programs	0	67	141
area, ethnic and cultural studies	3	117	184
biological sciences/life sciences	101	2,838	4,780
business and management	20	817	1,368
communications	5	232	338
communications technologies	0	0	7
computer and information sciences	9	367	867
education	218	5,128	6,676
engineering	89	2,507	6,369
engineering technologies	0	3	11
English language and literature/letters	32	1,240	1,535
foreign languages and literatures	64	499	876
health professions and related sciences	52	1,342	2,119
home economics	9	289	414
law and legal studies	3	40	91
liberal/general studies	1	61	75
library science	1	39	53
mathematics	9	547	1,209
multi/interdisciplinary studies	11	301	441
parks, recreation, and fitness studies	2	71	104
philosophy and religion	8	436	549
physical sciences	68	2,446	4,571
precision production trades	0	0	0
protective services	0	32	38
psychology	148	3,087	3,711
public administration and services	14	340	499
military technologies	0	0	0
social sciences and history	95	2,471	3,760
theological studies/religious vocations	10	1,062	1,521
transportation	0	0	0
visual and performing arts	16	802	1,067

SOURCE: U.S. Department of Education, Center for Education Statistics, <u>Digest of Education Statistics, 1998</u>, p. 343, table 272. ED 1.113\998

NOTES: 'Total' includes other races and ethnic groups not shown separately. 'White' excludes Hispanic persons.

UNITS: Earned Doctor's degrees conferred in number of degrees.

Table 5.15 First Professional Degrees Conferred, by Field of Study, 1994-95

	Hispanic	White	Total
All Fields, Total	3,476	59,456	76,641
Dentistry	177	2,516	3,697
Medicine	702	10,956	15,341
Optometry	47	911	1,231
Osteopathic medicine	74	1,529	1,895
Pharmacy	80	1,570	2,555
Podiatry	43	462	650
Veterinary medicine	77	1,935	2,109
Chiropractic medicine	113	2,777	3,379
Law	2,052	32,085	39,828
Theological professions	111	4,657	5,879

SOURCE: U.S. Department of Education, Center for Education Statistics, Digest of Education Statistics, 1998, p. 45, table 275.
ED 1.113\998

NOTES: 'Total' includes other races and ethnic groups not shown separately. 'White' excludes Hispanic persons.

UNITS: Earned first professional degrees conferred, in number of degrees.

Table 5.16 Educational Attainment: Years of School Completed by Persons 25 Years Old and Older, 1997

	Hispanic	White	Total
All persons 25 years old and over	15,476	144,058	170,581
percent of the population:			
not a high school graduate	45.3%	17.0%	17.9%
high school graduate	25.9	33.9	33.8
with some college, no degree	13.3	17.2	17.2
with associate's degree	5.2	7.4	7.3
with bachelor's degree	7.5	16.5	16.0
with advanced degree	2.9	8.1	7.8

SOURCE: U.S. Bureau of the Census, Statistical Abstract of the United States, 1998, p. 168, table 262. C 3.134:998

NOTES: 'Total' includes other races and ethnic groups not shown separately. Data as of March.

UNITS: Percent as a percent of the population 25 years old and older; number in thousands of persons 25 years old and older.

Table 5.17 College Completion, Persons 25 Years Old and Older, by Sex, 1970 - 1995

	Hispanic	White	Total
1970			
total	na%	11.6%	11.0%
men	na	15.0	14.1
women	na	8.6	8.2
1975			
total	6.3	14.5	13.9
men	8.3	18.4	17.6
women	4.6	11.0	10.6
1980			
total	7.9	17.8	17.0
men	9.7	22.1	20.9
women	6.2	14.0	13.6
1985			
total	8.5	16.0	19.4
men	9.7	20.0	23.1
women	7.3	24.0	16.0
1990			
total	9.2	22.0	21.3
men	9.8	25.3	24.4
women	8.7	19.0	18.4
1995			
total	9.3	24.0	23.0
men	10.1	27.2	26.0
women	8.4	21.0	20.2

SOURCE: U.S. Bureau of the Census, Current Population Reports: Educational Attainment in the United States: March 1995, Series P-20, #489, p. 91, table 18. C3.186/23:995 http://www.census.gov

NOTES: 'Total' includes other races and ethnic groups not shown separately.

UNITS: Percent as a percent of all persons 25 years old and older completing four or more years of college (1970-1991) or Bachelor's degree or more (1992 and later).

Table 5.18   Educational Attainment of the Hispanic Population, 25 Years Old and Over, by Type of Origin, 1985, 1990, 1997

	percent completing -				
	less than 5 years of school	4 years of high school or more	4 years of college or more	median years completed	all persons 25 years and over
1985					
Total resident population	2.7%	73.9%	19.4%	12.6	143,524
total Hispanic population	13.5	47.9	8.5	11.5	8,455
by origin					
Mexican origin	17.1	41.9	5.5	10.2	4,755
Puerto Rican origin	12.8	46.3	7.0	11.2	1,241
Cuban origin	7.4	51.1	13.7	12.0	721
Central/South American origin	7.2	62.6	15.5	12.4	951
other Hispanic origin	6.0	66.1	15.3	12.4	787
not of Hispanic origin	2.0	75.5	20.1	12.7	135,070
1990					
Total resident population	2.4%	77.6%	21.3%	na	156,538
total Hispanic population	12.3	50.8	9.2	na	10,832
by origin					
Mexican origin	15.5	44.1	5.4	na	6,424
Puerto Rican origin	9.7	55.5	9.7	na	1,169
Cuban origin	5.8	63.5	20.2	na	737
Central/South American origin	8.8	58.5	15.6	na	1,609
other Hispanic origin	3.9	68.7	15.2	na	894
not of Hispanic origin	1.7	79.6	22.2	na	145,705

continued on the next page

Table 5.18 continued

| | percent completing - | | | |
	less than 5 years of school	4 years of high school or more	4 years of college or more	all persons 25 years and over
1997				
Total resident population	1.7%	82.1%	16.0%	170,581
total Hispanic population	9.4	54.7	7.4	15,476
by origin				
Mexican origin	12.0	48.6	5.7	9,157
Puerto Rican origin	5.4	61.1	7.1	1,669
Cuban origin	6.0	65.2	12.1	946
Central/South American origin	5.7	63.3	10.7	2,473
other Hispanic origin	5.0	66.6	10.8	1,231
not of Hispanic origin	0.9	84.8	16.9	155,105

SOURCE: U.S. Bureau of the Census, The Hispanic Population in the United States: March, 1985, p. 12, table 1 (data from U.S. Bureau of the Census, *Current Population Reports*). C 3.186:P-20/422

U.S. Bureau of the Census, The Hispanic Population in the United States: March, 1990, pp. 6-7, table 1 (data from U.S. Bureau of the Census, *Current Population Reports*). C 3.186/14-2:990

U.S. Census Bureau, "Hispanic Population of the United States, (Tables 3.1, 3.2). March, 1997 CPS: Educational Attainment Level by Race-Ethnicity Age 25 and Over: Both Sexes- Values/Percents;", released 7 August 1998; <http://www.census.gov/population/socdemo/hispanic/cps97/tab03-1.txt> <http://www.census.gov/population/socdemo/hispanic/cps97/tab03-2.txt>

NOTES: Total population includes other races and ethnic groups not shown separately. 'Other Hispanic origin' includes persons from Spain and persons identifying themselves generally as Hispanic, Spanish, Spanish-American, Hispano, Latino, etc.

UNITS: Persons completing educational levels in percent as a percent of all persons, by origin, 100.0%; all persons 25 years and over in thousands of persons.

Table 5.19 Highest Educational Level and Degree Earned, Persons 18 Years Old and Older, 1997

	Hispanic	White	Total
Total civilian noninstitutional population	19,103	145,855	195,568
less than 7 years of elementary school	3,683	1,834	6,799
7 or 8 years of elementary school	1,324	4,860	7,250
1 to 3 years of high school	3,017	12,372	19,393
4 years of high school	607	1,584	2,868
high school graduate	5,005	50,200	65,370
some college	2,892	29,052	38,041
Associate degree	889	10,595	13,336
Bachelor's degree	1,228	24,072	29,089
Master's degree	282	7,731	9,205
First professional degree	103	2,076	2,455
Doctorate degree	73	1,477	1,761

SOURCE: U.S. Department of Education, Center for Education Statistics, Digest of Education Statistics, 1998, p. 4, table 9 (data from U.S. Bureau of the Census, *Current Population Reports*, unpublished data.) ED 1.113\998

NOTES: 'Total' includes other races and ethnic groups not shown separately. 'White' excludes persons of Hispanic origin.

UNITS: Persons in thousands, by highest educational level attained.

Table 5.20 Employment of 12th Graders, 1992

	Hispanic	White	Total
Most recent type of work for employed students, total	100.0%	100.0%	100.0%
lawn work or odd jobs	0.9	2.5	2.2
food service	24.8	22.8	24.0
delivery person	1.1	1.5	1.6
babysitter or child care	2.2	4.8	4.3
camp counselor/life guard	0.5	0.9	0.7
farm worker	1.1	2.7	2.2
mechanic	1.5	1.5	1.4
grocery clerk or cashier	11.6	14.8	14.5
beautician	0.3	0.1	0.2
house cleaning	2.0	0.8	0.9
construction	1.9	2.1	2.0
office or clerical	8.7	6.3	6.9
health services	1.1	1.6	1.6
salesperson	11.9	12.0	11.8
warehouse worker	1.7	2.2	2.1
other	28.8	23.5	23.5

SOURCE: U.S. Department of Education, Center for Education Statistics, Digest of Education Statistics, 1994, p. 403, table 373. Data from U.S. Department of Education, National Center for Education Statistics, "National Education Longitudianl Study of 1988,"Second Followup. ED 1.113\994

NOTES: 'Total' includes other races/ethnic groups not shown separately.

UNITS: Percent as a percent of all high school seniors of a given race/ethnicity who were employed in 1992.

Chapter 6: Government & Elections

Table 6.01 Hispanic Elected Public Officials, by Type of Office Held, 1985 - 1994

	State execut- ives & legislators	county & muni- cipal officials	judicial & law enforce- ment	educa- tion & school boards	total
1985	119	1,316	517	1,185	3,147
1986	122	1,352	530	1,188	3,202
1987	127	1,412	568	1,199	3,317
1988	124	1,425	574	1,226	3,360
1989	133	1,724	575	1,341	3,783
1990	134	1,819	583	1,458	4,004
1991	140	1,867	596	1,588	4,202
1992	139	1,908	628	2,308	4,994
1993	182	2,023	633	2,332	5,170
1994	199	2,197	651	2,412	5,459

SOURCE: U.S. Bureau of the Census, Statistical Abstract of the United States, 1995, p. 287, table 456 (data from National Association of Latino Elected and Appointed Officials, *National Roster of Hispanic Elected Officials*). C 3.134:995

NOTES: Data as of September. Total includes US Representatives not shown separately.

UNITS: Number of Hispanic elected public officials.

Table 6.02 Voting Age Population, Registration, and Voting, 1972 - 1996

	Hispanic	White	Total
Voting age population			
1972	5.6	121.2	136.2
1974	6.1	125.1	141.3
1976	6.6	129.3	146.5
1978	6.8	133.4	151.6
1980	8.8	137.7	157.1
1982	8.8	143.6	165.5
1984	9.5	146.8	170.0
1986	11.8	149.9	173.9
1988	12.9	152.8	178.1
1990	13.8	155.6	182.1
1992	14.7	157.8	185.7
1994	17.5	160.3	190.3
1996	18.4	162.8	193.7
Presidential election years			
percent reporting registration			
1972	44.4%	73.4%	72.3%
1976	37.8	68.3	66.7
1980	36.3	68.4	66.9
1984	40.1	69.6	68.3
1988	35.5	67.9	66.6
1992	35.0	70.1	68.2
1996	35.7	67.7	65.9
percent reporting voting			
1972	37.4%	64.5	63.0%
1976	31.8	60.9	59.2
1980	29.9	60.9	59.2
1984	32.6	61.4	59.9
1988	28.8	59.1	57.4
1992	28.9	63.6	61.3
1996	26.7	56.0	54.2

continued on the next page

Table 6.02   continued

	Hispanic	White	Total
Congressional election years			
percent reporting registration			
1974	34.9%	63.5%	62.6%
1978	32.9	63.8	62.6
1982	35.3	65.6	64.1
1986	35.9	65.3	64.3
1990	32.3	63.8	62.2
1994	31.3	64.6	62.5
percent reporting voting			
1974	22.9%	46.3%	44.7%
1978	23.5˙	47.3	45.9
1982	25.3	49.9	48.5
1986	24.2	47.0	46.0
1990	21.0	46.7	45.0
1994	20.2	47.3	45.0

SOURCE: U.S. Bureau of the Census, <u>Statistical Abstract of the United States,</u> <u>1989</u>, p. 257, table 432 (data from U.S. Bureau of the Census, *Current Population Reports*, Series P-20). C 3.134:989
U.S. Bureau of the Census, <u>Current Population Reports: Voting and</u> <u>Registration in the Election of November, 1988</u>, Series P-20, #440, pp. 48-49, table 8. C 3.186/3-2:989
U.S. Bureau of the Census, <u>Current Population Reports: Voting and</u> <u>Registration in the Election of November, 1990</u>, Series P-20, #453, pp. 16-17, table 2. C 3.186/3-2:990
U.S. Bureau of the Census, <u>Current Population Reports: Voting and</u> <u>Registration in the Election of November, 1992</u>, Series P-20, #466, pp. 4-5, table 2. C 3.186/3-2:992
Voting and Registration Data from the November 1994 Current Population Survey, Table 1, Table VI. http://www.census.gov
U.S. Bureau of the Census, <u>Current Population Reports: Voting and</u> <u>Registration in the Election of November, 1996</u>, Series P-20, #504, tabl 23. C 3.186/3-2:996

NOTES: 'Total' includes other races and ethnic groups not shown separately.

UNITS: Voting age population in millions of persons; percent reporting registration and percent reporting voting as a percent of the voting age population.

Table 6.03 Voting Age Population, Selected Characteristics, 1990

	Hispanic	White	Total
Voting age population, 1990			
by age			
total 18 years and over	13,756	155,587	182,118
18-20 years old	1,139	8,722	10,800
21-24 years old	1,572	11,635	14,031
25-34 years old	4,180	35,682	45,652
35-44 years old	2,886	32,281	37,889
45-54 years old	1,707	21,983	25,648
55-64 years old	1,200	18,477	21,223
65-74 years old	728	16,180	18,126
75 years and over	344	10,627	11,748
by sex			
male	6,787	74,625	86,621
female	6,968	80,962	95,496
by years of school completed			
elementary			
0-4 years of school	1,417	2,617	3,669
5-7 years of school	1,903	5,096	6,445
8 years of school	910	6,564	7,617
high school			
1-3 years high school	2,353	16,733	20,956
4 years high school	4,160	61,342	71,492
college			
1-3 years college	1,881	31,481	36,300
4 years college	679	18,900	21,350
5 or more years college	452	12,855	14,288
by family income			
under $5,000	801	4,503	6,799
$5,000-$9,999	1,425	6,978	9,808
$10,000-$14,999	1,877	11,049	13,759
$15,000-$19,999	1,185	8,677	10,496
$20,000-$24,999	1,162	10,619	12,304
$25,000-$34,999	1,832	20,827	23,627
$35,000-$49,999	1,384	22,698	25,367
$50,000 and over	1,231	30,330	32,818
income not reported	768	9,555	11,576

SOURCE: U.S. Bureau of the Census, <u>Current Population Reports: Voting and Registration in the Election of November, 1990</u>, Series P-20, #453, pp. 16-17, table 2; pp. 47-48, table 8; p. 64, table 13.
C 3.186/3-2:990

NOTES: 'Total' includes other races and ethnic groups not shown separately.

UNITS: Voting age population in thousands of persons.

Table 6.04 Selected Characteristics of Persons Registered to Vote, 1990

	Hispanic	White	Total
Persons registered to vote, 1990			
by age			
total 18 years and over	32.3%	63.8%	62.2%
18-20 years old	17.2	37.0	35.4
21-24 years old	20.9	43.1	43.3
25-34 years old	27.4	53.2	52.0
35-44 years old	34.8	67.2	65.5
45-54 years old	38.3	71.3	69.8
55-64 years old	45.5	74.9	73.5
65-74 years old	56.6	79.7	78.3
75 years and over	46.0	74.8	73.7
by sex			
male	30.0%	63.0%	61.2%
female	34.5	64.6	63.1
by years of school completed			
elementary			
0-4 years of school	15.3%	26.4%	29.5%
5-7 years of school	15.8	38.7	41.1
8 years of school	28.1	54.3	53.3
high school			
1-3 years high school	24.6	48.2	47.9
4 years high school	36.6	61.2	60.0
college			
1-3 years college	50.6	70.2	68.7
4 years college	51.1	77.1	74.5
5 or more years college	59.3	83.5	81.5
by households income			
under $5,000	28.2%	53.1%	50.7%
$5,000-$9,999	22.7	47.6	48.3
$10,000-$14,999	23.9	55.4	54.8
$15,000-$19,999	29.0	57.5	56.8
$20,000-$24,999	21.7	59.0	58.0
$25,000-$34,999	37.7	65.0	63.9
$35,000-$49,999	46.5	69.4	68.3
$50,000 and over	51.7	77.8	76.4
income not reported	29.6	59.7	57.6

SOURCE: U.S. Bureau of the Census, Current Population Reports: Voting and Registration in the Election of November, 1990, Series P-20, #453, pp. 16-17, table 2; pp. 47-48, table 8; p. 64, table 13. C 3.186/3-2:990

NOTES: 'Total' includes other races and ethnic groups not shown separately.

UNITS: Person reporting registration to vote as a percent of the voting age population, 100.0%.

Table 6.05   Selected Characteristics of Persons Voting, 1990

	Hispanic	White	Total
Persons voting, 1990			
by age			
total 18 years and over	21.0%	46.7%	45.0%
18-20 years old	10.1	19.4	18.4
21-24 years old	7.8	21.8	22.0
25-34 years old	16.5	34.9	33.8
35-44 years old	24.2	50.0	48.4
45-54 years old	25.4	54.9	53.2
55-64 years old	33.5	60.4	58.9
65-74 years old	43.8	65.7	64.1
75 years and over	33.4	55.8	54.5
by sex			
male	19.4%	46.4%	44.6%
female	22.6	46.9	45.4
by years of school completed			
elementary			
0-4 years of school	9.4%	14.8%	16.5%
5-7 years of school	11.3	23.7	25.7
8 years of school	15.6	35.7	34.8
high school			
1-3 years high school	13.5	31.3	30.9
4 years high school	22.5	43.6	42.2
college			
1-3 years college	36.0	51.4	50.0
4 years college	38.8	61.6	59.0
5 or more years college	45.8	69.6	67.8
by households income			
under $5,000	14.9%	35.1%	32.2%
$5,000-$9,999	14.6	31.3	30.9
$10,000-$14,999	14.5	38.5	37.7
$15,000-$19,999	16.6	39.9	38.8
$20,000-$24,999	14.9˙	42.5	41.3
$25,000-$34,999	26.3	47.5	46.4
$35,000-$49,999	29.8	51.8	51.0
$50,000 and over	37.8	60.5	59.2
income not reported	19.3	45.1	43.3

SOURCE: U.S. Bureau of the Census, Current Population Reports: Voting and Registration in the Election of November, 1990, Series P-20, #453, pp. 16-17, table 2; pp. 47-48, table 8; p. 64, table 13.
C 3.186/3-2:990

NOTES: 'Total' includes other races and ethnic groups not shown separately.

UNITS: Persons reporting voting as a percent of the voting age population, 100.0%.

Table 6.06   Voting Age Population, Selected Characteristics, 1996

	Hispanic	White	Total
Voting age population, 1996			
by age			
total 18 years and over	18,426	162,779	193,651
18-20 years old	1,421	8,641	10,785
21-24 years old	2,031	11,028	13,865
25-34 years old	5,228	32,632	40,066
35-44 years old	4,322	36,000	43,327
45-54 years old	2,310	27,793	32,684
55-64 years old	1,626	18,228	21,037
65-74 years old	1,003	16,080	18,176
75 years and over	485	12,376	13,712
by sex			
male	9,213	78,654	92,632
female	9,213	84,125	101,020
by years of school completed			
less than 5th grade	1,448	2,194	3,069
5th to 8th grade	3,189	9,142	10,917
9th to 12th grade,			
no diploma	3,494	16,508	21,002
high school graduate	5,154	54,924	65,208
some college or			
associate degree	3,480	42,983	50,939
bachelor's degree	1,217	25,064	28,829
advanced degree	442	11,965	13,688
by labor force status			
in civilian labor force	12,947	111,332	132,043
employed	11,961	106,660	125,634
unemployed	986	4,672	6,409

continued on the next page

Table 6.06   continued

	Hispanic	White	Total
by occupation			
managerial and professional	1,640	32,947	37,462
technical, sales, and			
administrative support	3,058	31,504	36,973
service occupations	2,385	12,576	16,238
farming, forestry, fishing	611	2,960	3,171
precision production, craft			
and repair	1,557	12,077	13,647
operators, fabricators, laborers	2,711	14,596	18,143
by family income			
under $5,000	780	2,169	3,590
$5,000-$9,999	1,398	4,163	6,302
$10,000-$14,999	2,115	7,861	10,281
$15,000-$24,999	3,116	15,551	19,135
$25,000-$34,999	2,454	17,067	20,187
$35,000-$49,999	1,919	22,013	25,319
$50,000-$74.999	1,364	24,490	27,451
$75,000 and over	853	21,170	23,348
income not reported	864	11,727	13,875

SOURCE: U.S. Bureau of the Census, Current Population Reports: Voting and Registration in the Election of November, 1996, Series P-20, #504, pp. 4-5, table 2; pp. 39-40, table 8; pp. 47-54, tables 10, 11; p. 56, table 13. <www.census.gov/prod/3/98pubs/p20-504u.pdf>, accessed 15 October 1998.

NOTES: 'Total' includes other races and ethnic groups not shown separately.

UNITS: Voting age population in thousands of persons.

Table 6.07 Selected Characteristics of Persons Registered to Vote, 1996

	Hispanic	White	Total
Persons registered to vote, 1996			
by age			
total 18 years and over	6,573	110,259	127,651
18-20 years old	386	4,078	4,919
21-24 years old	567	5,722	7,099
25-34 years old	1,454	18,997	22,778
35-44 years old	1,580	24,675	28,828
45-54 years old	999	20,530	23,559
55-64 years old	781	14,043	15,930
65-74 years old	532	12,745	14,218
75 years and over	275	9,470	10,329
by sex			
male	3,028	52,218	59,672
female	3,545	58,041	67,989
by years of school completed			
less than 5th grade	285	582	872
5th to 8th grade	569	3,974	4,825
9th to 12th grade, no diploma	954	7,809	10,059
high school graduate	1,950	34,999	40,542
some college or associate degree	1,812	32,099	37,160
bachelor's degree	705	20,424	22,752
advanced degree	298	10,373	11,451
by labor force status			
in civilian labor force	4,665	75,428	87,532
employed	4,400	72,998	84,166
unemployed	265	2,430	3,365

continued on the next page

Table 6.07   continued

	Hispanic	White	Total
by occupation			
managerial and professional	1,019	26,852	29,889
technical, sales, and			
administrative support	1,575	22,772	26,068
service occupations	643	7,075	9,083
farming, forestry, fishing	82	1,787	1,893
precision production, craft			
and repair	419	6,937	7,811
operators, fabricators, laborers	662	7,575	9,423
by family income			
under $5,000	233	964	1,719
$5,000-$9,999	355	1,876	3,025
$10,000-$14,999	517	4,156	5,494
$15,000-$24,999	853	9,235	11,169
$25,000-$34,999	930	11,263	13,059
$35,000-$49,999	912	16,090	18,008
$50,000-$74,999	784	19,230	21,169
$75,000 and over	596	17,778	19,243
income not reported	214	6,748	7,712

SOURCE: U.S. Bureau of the Census, Current Population Reports: Voting and Registration in the Election of November, 1996, Series P-20, #504, pp. 4-5, table 2; pp. 39-40, table 8; pp. 47-54, tables 10, 11; p. 56, table 13. <www.census.gov/prod/3/98pubs/p20-504u.pdf>, accessed 15 October 1998.

NOTES: 'Total' includes other races and ethnic groups not shown separately.

UNITS: Voting age population in thousands of persons.

Table 6.08   Selected Characteristics of Persons Voting, 1996

	Hispanic	White	Total
Persons voting, 1996			
by age			
total 18 years and over	4,928	91,208	105,017
18-20 years old	228	2,808	3,366
21-24 years old	294	3,748	4,630
25-34 years old	1,026	14,426	17,265
35-44 years old	1,163	20,432	23,785
45-54 years old	830	17,786	20,360
55-64 years old	677	12,629	14,255
65-74 years old	489	11,477	12,748
75 years and over	220	7,903	8,608
by sex			
male	2,233	43,111	48,909
female	2,695	48,097	56,108
by years of school completed			
less than 5th grade	229	408	618
5th to 8th grade	447	2,928	3,570
9th to 12th grade,			
no diploma	627	5,535	7,099
high school graduate	1,313	27,802	32,019
some college or			
associate degree	1,406	26,643	30,835
bachelor's degree	625	18,257	20,256
advanced degree	282	9,637	10,621
by labor force status			
in civilian labor force	3,469	62,059	71,682
employed	3,297	60,303	69,300
unemployed	171	1,755	2,383

continued on the next page

Table 6.08   continued

	Hispanic	White	Total
by occupation			
managerial and professional	860	23,606	26,309
technical, sales, and			
administrative support	1,180	18,870	21,530
service occupations	463	5,465	6,992
farming, forestry, fishing	62	1,479	1,557
precision production, craft			
and repair	273	5,320	5,988
operators, fabricators, laborers	460	5,563	6,923
by family income			
under $5,000	136	631	1,179
$5,000-$9,999	250	1,269	2,064
$10,000-$14,999	355	3,078	4,057
$15,000-$19,999	613	7,234	8,778
$20,000-$24,999	679	9,095	10,499
$25,000-$34,999	671	13,466	15,037
$35,000-$49,999	646	16,694	18,347
$50,000 and over	507	15,883	17,177
income not reported	191	5,835	6,598

SOURCE: U.S. Bureau of the Census, Current Population Reports: Voting and Registration in the Election of November, 1996, Series P-20, #504, pp. 4-5, table 2; pp. 39-40, table 8; pp. 47-54, tables 10, 11; p. 56, table 13. <www.census.gov/prod/3/98pubs/p20-504u.pdf>, accessed 15 October 1998.

NOTES: 'Total' includes other races and ethnic groups not shown separately.

UNITS: Voting age population in thousands of persons.

Table 6.09 Members of Congress, 1981 - 1995

	Hispanic	White	Total
House of Representatives			
97th Congress, 1981	6	415	435
98th Congress, 1983	8	411	"
99th Congress, 1985	10	412	"
100th Congress, 1987	11	408	"
101st Congress, 1989	10	406	"
102nd Congress, 1991	11	407	"
103rd Congress, 1993	17	393	"
104th Congress, 1995	17	391	"
Senate			
97th Congress, 1981	0	97	100
98th Congress, 1983	0	98	"
99th Congress, 1985	0	98	"
100th Congress, 1987	0	98	"
101st Congress, 1989	0	98	"
102nd Congress, 1991	0	98	"
103rd Congress, 1993	0	97	"
104th Congress, 1995	0	97	"

SOURCE: U.S. Bureau of the Census, <u>Statistical Abstract of the United States, 1995</u>, p. 281, table 444 (data from Congressional Quarterly, Inc.). C 3.134:995

NOTES: 'Total' includes other races and ethnic groups not shown separately.

UNITS: Number of members of the House and Senate respectively, as shown.

Chapter 7: The Labor Force, Employment & Unemployment

Table 7.01 Labor Force Participation of the Civilian Noninstitutional
Population 16 Years Old & Over, by Age, 1985, 1990, 1997

	Hispanic	White	Total
1985			
civilian noninstitutional population all persons 16 years old and over	11,915	153,679	178,206
- persons 16-19 years old	1,298	11,900	14,506
- persons 20 years old and over	10,617	141,780	163,700
- persons 65 years old and over	843	24,352	26,977
civilian labor force all persons 16 years old and over	7,698	99,926	115,461
- persons 16-19 years old	579	6,841	7,901
- persons 20 years old and over	7,119	93,085	107,560
- persons 65 years old and over	82	2,605	2,907
labor force participation rate all persons 16 years old and over	64.6%	65.0%	64.8%
- persons 16-19 years old	44.6	57.5	54.5
- persons 20 years old and over	67.1	65.7	65.7
- persons 65 years old and over	9.7	10.7	10.8

continued on the next page

Table 7.01   continued

	Hispanic	White	Total
1990			
civilian noninstitutional population			
all persons 16 years old and over	14,297	160,415	188,049
- persons 16-19 years old	1,424	11,095	13,794
- persons 20 years old and over	12,873	149,320	174,255
- persons 65 years old and over	na	26,643	29,730
civilian labor force			
all persons 16 years old and over	9576	107,177	124,787
- persons 16-19 years old	672	6,374	7,410
- persons 20 years old and over	8,904	100,803	117,377
- persons 65 years old and over	na	3,189	3,535
labor force participation rate			
all persons 16 years old and over	67.0%	66.8%	66.4%
- persons 16-19 years old	47.2	57.5	53.7
- persons 20 years old and over	69.2	62.8	62.4
- persons 65 years old and over	na	12.0	11.9

continued on the next page

Table 7.01   continued

	Hispanic	White	Total
1997			
civilian noninstitutional population			
all persons 16 years old and over	20,321	169,993	203,133
- persons 16-19 years old	2,121	12,181	15,365
- persons 65 years old and over	1,558	28,514	31,989
civilian labor force			
all persons 16 years old and over	13,796	114,693	136,297
- persons 16-19 years old	911	6,720	7,932
- persons 65 years old and over	186	3,517	3,887
labor force participation rate			
all persons 16 years old and over	67.9%	67.5%	67.1%
- persons 16-19 years old	43.0	55.2	51.6
- persons 65 years old and over	11.9	12.3	12.2

SOURCE: U.S. Department of Labor, Bureau of Labor Statistics, Handbook of Labor Statistics, 1989, pp. 13-30, tables 3-5. L 2.3/5:989
U.S. Department of Labor, Bureau of Labor Statistics, *Employment and Earnings*, January, 1991, p. 208, table 39; January, 1998, p. 164-165, table 3, p. 167, table 4 (data from the Current Population Survey). L2.41/2:(vol)/1:(year)

NOTES: 'Total' includes other races and ethnic groups not shown separately.

UNITS: Civilian noninstitutional population and civilian labor force in thousands of persons; participation rate as a percent (the civilian noninstitutional population divided by the civilian labor force).

Table 7.02 Labor Force Participation of the Civilian Noninstitutional Population 16 Years Old and Over, by Sex and Age, 1985, 1990, 1997

	Hispanic		White		Total	
	male	female	male	female	male	female
1985						
civilian noninstitutional population						
all persons 16 years old and over	5,885	6,029	73,373	80,306	84,469	93,736
- persons 16-19 years old	654	644	5,987	5,912	7,275	7,231
- persons 20 years old and over	5,232	5,385	67,386	74,394	77,195	86,506
- persons 65 years old and over	354	489	10,010	14,342	11,084	15,913
civilian labor force						
all persons 16 years old and over	4,729	2,970	56,472	43,455	64,411	51,050
- persons 16-19 years old	334	245	3,576	3,265	4,134	3,767
- persons 20 years old and over	4,395	2,725	52,895	40,190	60,277	47,283
- persons 65 years old and over	53	29	1,595	1,010	1,750	1,156
labor force participation rate						
all persons 16 years old and over	80.3%	49.3%	77.0%	54.1%	76.3%	54.5%
- persons 16-19 years old	51.0	38.1	59.7	55.2	56.8	52.1
- persons 20 years old and over	84.0	50.6	78.5	54.0	78.1	54.7
- persons 65 years old and over	14.9	5.9	15.9	7.0	15.8	7.3

continued on the next page

Table 7.02   continued

	Hispanic		White		Total	
	male	female	male	female	male	female
1990						
civilian noninstitutional population						
all persons 16 years old and over	7,087	7,210	77,082	83,332	89,650	98,399
- persons 16-19 years old	721	703	5,600	5,495	6,947	6,847
- persons 20 years old and over	6,366	6,507	71,482	77,837	82,703	91,552
- persons 65 years old and over	na	na	11,129	15,514	12,392	17,337
civilian labor force						
all persons 16 years old and over	5,755	3,821	58,298	47,879	68,234	56,554
- persons 16-19 years old	401	271	3,329	3,046	3,866	3,544
- persons 20 years old and over	5,354	3,550	54,969	44,833	64,368	53,010
- persons 65 years old and over	na	na	1,865	1,325	2,033	1,502
labor force participation rate						
all persons 16 years old and over	81.2%	53.0%	76.9%	57.5%	76.1%	57.5%
- persons 16-19 years old	55.6	38.5	59.4	55.4	55.7	51.8
- persons 20 years old and over	84.1	54.6	78.3	57.6	77.8	57.9
- persons 65 years old and over	na	na	16.8	8.5	16.4	8.7

continued on the next page

Table 7.02   continued

	Hispanic		White		Total	
1997	male	female	male	female	male	female
civilian noninstitutional population						
all persons 16 years old and over	10,368	9,953	82,577	87,417	97,715	105,418
- persons 16-19 years old	1,119	1,003	6,257	5,924	7,836	7,528
- persons 65 years old and over	651	907	12,067	16,447	13,469	18,520
civilian labor force						
all persons 16 years old and over	8,309	5,486	62,639	52,054	73,261	63,036
- persons 16-19 years old	531	381	3,513	3,207	4,095	3,837
- persons 65 years old and over	113	73	2,094	1,422	2,298	1,590
labor force participation rate						
all persons 16 years old and over	80.1%	55.1%	75.9%	59.5%	75.0%	59.8%
- persons 16-19 years old	47.4	38.0	56.1	54.1	52.3	51.0
- persons 65 years old and over	17.3	8.1	17.4	8.6	17.1	8.6

SOURCE: U.S. Department of Labor, Bureau of Labor Statistics, Handbook of Labor Statistics, 1989, pp. 13-30, tables 3-5. L 2.3/5:989
U.S. Department of Labor, Bureau of Labor Statistics, *Employment and Earnings*, January, 1991, p. 208, table 39; January, 1998, p. 164-165, table 3, p. 167, table 4 (data from the Current Population Survey). L 2.41/2:(vol)/1:(year)

NOTES: 'Total' includes other races and ethnic groups not shown separately.

UNITS: Civilian noninstitutional population and civilian labor force in thousands of persons; participation rate as a percent (the civilian noninstitutional population divided by the civilian labor force).

Table 7.03 Labor Force Participation of the Hispanic Civilian Noninstitutional Population 16 Years Old and Over, by Type of Hispanic Origin, 1985, 1990, 1997

	Mexican	Puerto Rican	Cuban	Central/ South Amer	other Hispanic	total Hispanic
1985						
Total population 16 years old and over						
number	6,625	1,721	851	1,248	1,021	11,446
percent	100.0%	100.0%	100.0%	100.0%	100.0%	100.0%
in labor force						
number	4,427	882	557	853	643	7,362
percent	66.8%	51.2%	65.5%	68.3%	63.0%	64.2%
Male population 16 years old and over						
number	3,402	754	413	587	486	5,643
percent	100.0%	100.0%	100.0%	100.0%	100.0%	100.0%
in the labor force						
number	2,773	504	308	483	358	4,427
percent	81.5%	66.9%	74.6%	82.3%	73.7%	78.5%
Female population 16 years old and over						
number	3,223	967	438	661	534	5,823
percent	100.0%	100.0%	100.0%	100.0%	100.0%	100.0%
in the labor force						
number	1,654	378	249	370	584	2,935
percent	51.3%	39.0%	56.9%	55.9%	53.2%	50.4%

continued on the next page

Table 7.03   continued

	type of origin					
	Mexican	Puerto Rican	Cuban	Central/ South Amer	other Hispanic	total Hispanic
1990						
Total population						
16 years old and over						
number	8,696	1,492	839	2,106	1,079	114,212
percent	100.0%	100.0%	100.0%	100.0%	100.0%	100.0%
in labor force						
number	5,871	805	554	1,509	709	9,449
percent	67.5%	54.0%	66.0%	71.7%	65.7%	66.5%
Male population						
16 years old and over						
number	4,493	673	402	991	511	7,069
percent	100.0%	100.0%	100.0%	100.0%	100.0%	100.0%
in the labor force						
number	3,647	466	301	829	385	5,629
percent	81.2%	69.2%	74.9%	83.7%	75.3%	79.6%
Female population						
16 years old and over						
number	4,203	819	438	1,114	568	7,143
percent	100.0%	100.0%	100.0%	100.0%	100.0%	100.0%
in the labor force						
number	2,224	339	253	680	324	3,821
percent	52.9%	41.4%	57.8%	61.0%	57.0%	53.5%
1997						
Total population						
16 years old and over						
number	12,249	2,134	1,049	3,190	1,563	20,184
percent	100.0%	100.0%	100.0%	100.0%	100.0%	100.0%
in labor force						
number	8,369	1,228	651	2,251	1,009	13,509
percent	68.3%	57.6%	62.1%	70.6%	64.6%	66.9%

continued on the next page

Table 7.03   continued

| | | | | type of origin | | |
	Mexican	Puerto Rican	Cuban	Central/ South Amer	other Hispanic	total Hispanic
1997 - continued						
Male population						
16 years old and over						
number	6,476	967	560	1,574	747	10,324
percent	100.0%	100.0%	100.0%	100.0%	100.0%	100.0%
in the labor force						
number	5,251	656	392	1,286	545	8,129
percent	81.1%	67.8%	70.0%	81.7%	72.9%	78.7%
Female population						
16 years old and over						
number	5,773	1,167	490	1,616	815	9,860
percent	100.0%	100.0%	100.0%	100.0%	100.0%	100.0%
in the labor force						
number	3,119	572	260	965	464	5,380
percent	54.0%	49.0%	53.0%	59.7%	56.9%	54.6%

SOURCE: U.S. Bureau of the Census, The Hispanic Population in the United States: March, 1985, pp. 14-15, table 2 (data from U.S. Bureau of the Census, *Current Population Reports*). C 3.186:P-20/422
U.S. Bureau of the Census, The Hispanic Population in the United States: March, 1990, pp. 8-9, table 2 (data from U.S. Bureau of the Census, *Current Population Reports*). C 3.186/14-2:990
U.S. Bureau of the Census, Hispanic Population from the March, 1994 Current Population Survey. Released on Internet only. http://www.census.gov
U.S. Census Bureau, "Hispanic Population of the United States, (Table 7.1). March, 1997 CPS: Civilian Labor For Status by Race-Ethnicity Age 16 and Over: By Sex - Values/Percents;", released 7 August 1998; <http://www.census.gov/population/socdemo/hispanic/cps97/tab07-1.txt>

NOTES: 'Other Hispanic origin' includes persons from Spain and persons identifying themselves generally as Hispanic, Spanish, Spanish-American, Hispano, Latino, etc.

UNITS: Total population in thousands of persons 16 years old and over; percent as a percent of total shown (100.0%).

Table 7.04 Civilian Labor Force and Civilian Labor Force Participation
Rates: Projections for 2006

	Hispanic	White	Total
2006			
civilian labor force			
total	17.4%	123.6%	148.8%
men	10.2	66.0	78.2
women	7.2	57.6	70.6
labor force participation rate			
total	67.4%	68.1%	67.6%
men	77.1	74.3	73.6
women	57.2	62.0	61.4

SOURCE: U.S. Bureau of the Census, Statistical Abstract of the United States, 1998, p. 403, table 645 (data from U.S. Department of Labor, Bureau of Labor Statistics) C 3.134:998

NOTES: 'Total' includes other races and ethnic groups not shown separately.

UNITS: Civilian labor force population 16 years old and over in millions of persons; labor force participation rate as a percent (the civilian noninstitutional population divided by the civilian labor force).

Table 7.05 Employed Members of the Civilian Labor Force, by Sex and Age, 1985, 1990, 1997

	Hispanic		White		Total	
	male	female	male	female	male	female
1985						
all employed persons 16 years old and over	4,245	2,642	53,046	40,690	59,891	47,259
- persons 16-19 years old	251	187	2,985	2,783	3,328	3,105
- persons 20 years old and over	3,994	2,456	50,061	37,907	56,562	44,154
- persons 65 years old and over	48	27	1,552	978	1,695	1,118
1990						
all employed persons 16 years old and over	5,304	3,504	56,432	45,654	64,435	53,479
- persons 16-19 years old	323	218	2,856	2,662	3,237	3,024
- persons 20 years old and over	4,981	3,286	53,576	42,992	61,198	50,455
- persons 65 years old and over	na	na	1,812	1,288	1,972	1,455
1997						
all employed persons 16 years old and over	7,728	4,999	59,998	49,859	69,685	59,873
- persons 16-19 years old	420	294	3,011	2,796	3,401	3,260
- persons 65 years old and over	105	69	2,037	1,374	2,229	1,532

SOURCE: U.S. Department of Labor, Bureau of Labor Statistics, Handbook of Labor Statistics, 1989, pp. 63-68, table 15, (data from the Current Population Survey). L 2.3/5:989
U.S. Department of Labor, Bureau of Labor Statistics, *Employment and Earnings*, January, 1991, pp. 208, table 39 January, 1998, pp. 164-165, table 3, p. 167, table 4 (data from the Current Population Survey). L 2.41/2:(vol)/1:(year)

NOTES: 'Total' includes other races and ethnic groups not shown separately. Data covers members of the civilian labor force.

UNITS: Employed members of the civilian labor force in thousands of persons, by age group as shown.

Table 7.06 Employed Hispanic Persons as Percent of All Employed Persons in the Civilian Labor Force, by Selected Occupation, 1997

1997

All occupations	9.8%
Managerial and professional specialty	5.0
executive, administrative and managerial	5.4
Professional specialty	4.5
architects	5.1
engineers	3.8
mathematical and computer scientists	3.1
natural scientists	2.2
physicians	4.8
dentists	1.1
health assessment and treatment occupations	3.3
college and university teachers	3.4
teachers, except college and university	5.4
lawyers and judges	3.8
writers, artists, entertainers, and athletes	5.8
Technicians, sales, and administrative support	7.9
technical and related support	6.1
health technologists	6.3
engineering and related technologists and technicians	6.7
science technicians	8.3
Sales occupations	7.6
Administrative support, including clerical	8.6
computer equipment operators	7.0
secretaries, stenographers, typists	6.9

continued on the next page

Table 7.06   continued

Service occupations	14.6%
private household	26.6
protective service	8.8
fire fighting and fire prevention	5.7
police and detectives	7.6
guards	11.0
Service occupations (except private household and protective service)	14.9
food preparation and service occupations	16.4
health service occupations	9.2
cleaning and building service occupations	21.3
personal service occupations	9.6
Precision production, craft and repair	12.1
mechanics and repairers	10.2
construction trades	13.7
precision production occupations	12.2
Operators, fabricators, and laborers	15.4
machine operators, assemblers, and inspectors	17.9
Transportation and material moving occupations	11.0
Handlers, equipment cleaners, helpers, and laborers	16.3
Farming, forestry, and fishing	20.6
farm operators and managers	2.4

SOURCE: U.S. Department of Labor, Bureau of Labor Statistics, *Employment and Earnings*, January, 1998, pp. 174-179, table 11 (data from the Current Population Survey). L 2.41/2:40/1:998

NOTES: Only selected subcategories of occupational groups displayed.

UNITS: Employed Hispanic persons as a percent of all employed persons, by occupation.

Table 7.07 Employed Hispanic Persons, by Occupation, as Percent of All Employed Hispanic Persons, by Sex, by Type of Hispanic Origin, 1990 and 1997

				type of origin		
	Mexican	Puerto Rican	Cuban	Central/ South Amer	other Hispanic	total Hispanic
1990						
All employed males						
number	3,335	428	282	772	361	5,178
percent	100.0%	100.0%	100.0%	100.0%	100.0%	100.0%
by occupation						
managerial and professional						
specialty	8.3%	11.2%	25.9%	12.2%	16.6%	10.7%
technicians, sales, and						
administrative support	12.6	19.4	20.2	17.1	18.6	14.7
service occupations	15.1	20.6	11.3	19.8	17.7	16.2
farming, forestry, and fishing	11.2	2.6	1.3	2.6	2.8	8.0
precision production,						
craft and repair	21.2	22.0	20.9	17.0	21.1	20.6
operators, fabricators,						
and laborers	31.7	24.5	20.9	31.3	23.3	29.6
All employed females						
number	2,006	308	240	637	305	3,496
percent	100.0%	100.0%	100.0%	100.0%	100.0%	100.0%
by occupation						
managerial and professional						
specialty	14.2%	23.1%	22.1%	14.1%	20.3%	16.0%
technicians, sales, and						
administrative support	38.1	43.5	47.5	31.4	42.3	38.4
service occupations	23.9	18.8	18.3	35.0	23.6	25.1
farming, forestry, and fishing	1.8	0.3	0.4	0.0	0.3	1.1
precision production,						
craft and repair	3.2	1.9	1.3	1.9	2.6	2.7
operators, fabricators,						
and laborers	18.8	12.0	10.4	17.4	10.5	16.6

continued on the next page

Table 7.07 continued

	Mexican	Puerto Rican	Cuban	Central/ South Amer	other Hispanic	total Hispanic
1997						
All employed males						
number	4,772	562	367	1,199	485	7,385
percent	100.0%	100.0%	100.0%	100.0%	100.0%	100.0%
by occupation						
managerial and professional	9.6%	11.7%	25.4%	14.7%	19.5%	12.0%
technical, sales, and administrative support	12.8	19.8	21.4	16.4	22.6	15.0
service	16.0	23.1	15.2	20.4	13.0	17.0
precision production, craft and repair	21.2	18.0	14.3	16.3	18.6	19.7
operators, fabricators, and laborers	29.2	26.6	20.9	27.2	22.3	27.8
farming, forestry, and fishing	11.2	0.7	2.7	5.0	3.9	8.5
All employed females						
number	2,801	526	245	897	408	4,877
percent	100.0%	100.0%	100.0%	100.0%	100.0%	100.0%
by occupation						
managerial and professional	16.3%	25.5%	24.0%	19.3%	22.0%	18.7%
technical, sales, and administrative support	37.5	40.7	45.1	32.8	40.5	37.6
service	24.7	21.9	22.2	28.7	25.2	25.0
precision production, craft and repair	2.7	1.5	1.6	1.9	1.7	2.3
operators, fabricators, and laborers	16.6	9.8	7.0	17.0	10.6	15.0
farming, forestry, and fishing	2.1	0.6	0.0	0.5	0.0	1.4

SOURCE: U.S. Bureau of the Census, The Hispanic Population in the United States: March, 1990, pp. 8-9, table 2 (data from U.S. Bureau of the Census, *Current Population Reports*). C 3.186/14-2:990
U.S. Bureau of the Census, The Hispanic Population in the United States: March, 1992, pp. 13-15, table 2 (data from U.S. Bureau of the Census, *Current Population Reports*). C 3.186/14-2:992
U.S. Census Bureau, "Hispanic Population of the United States, (Table 9.2). March, 1997 CPS: Occupation by Race-Ethnicity Employed Persons Age 16 and Over: Males - Values/Percents;", "Hispanic Population of the United States, (Table 9.3). March, 1997 CPS: Occupation by Race-Ethnicity Employed Persons Age 16 and Over: Females - Values/Percents;", released 7 August 1998;
<http://www.census.gov/population/socdemo/hispanic/cps97/tab09-2.txt>
<http://www.census.gov/population/socdemo/hispanic/cps97/tab09-3.txt>

NOTES: Total population includes other races and ethnic groups not shown separately. 'Other Hispanic origin' includes persons from Spain and persons identifying themselves generally as Hispanic, Spanish, Spanish-American, Hispano, Latino, etc.

UNITS: Employed persons in thousands of persons 16 years old and over; percent as a percent of total shown (100.0%).

Table 7.08 Employed Hispanic Persons as Percent of All Employed Persons in the Civilian Labor Force, by Industry Group, 1997

1997

All industries	9.8%
agriculture	19.4
mining	9.4
construction	11.8
manufacturing	11.2
transportation, communications, and other public utilities	8.6
wholesale and retail trade	11.1
wholesale trade	10.7
retail trade	11.2
finance, insurance and real estate	7.2
services	8.5
public administration	6.5

SOURCE: U.S. Department of Labor, Bureau of Labor Statistics, *Employment and Earnings*, January, 1998, p. 184-187, table 18 (data from Current Population Survey). L 2.41/2:40/1:997

NOTES: Only selected subcategories of industry groups are displayed.

UNITS: Employed Hispanic persons as a percent of all employed persons, by industry group.

Table 7.09   Full-Time and Part-Time Status of the Labor Force, by Region, 1996

	Hispanic	White	Total
1996			
Northeast			
Employed persons			
Full-time workers, total	1,374	16,859	19,598
35 hours of more	1,191	14,265	16,632
at work 1 to 34 hours			
for economic reasons	18	185	186
not at work	50	778	863
Part-time workers, total	234	4,227	4,718
at work for economic reasons	53	515	625
not at work	12	311	343
Unemployed persons			
Looking for full-time work	156	867	1,176
Looking for part-time work	29	224	272
Midwest			
Employed persons			
Full-time workers, total	750	22,398	24,929
35 hours of more	672	19,456	21,628
at work 1 to 34 hours			
for economic reasons	8	272	303
not at work	22	879	1,001
Part-time workers, total	127	5,690	6,188
at work for economic reasons	29	514	598
not at work	5	385	416
Unemployed persons			
Looking for full-time work	63	843	1,130
Looking for part-time work	13	289	339

continued on the next page

Table 7.09   continued

	Hispanic	White	Total
South			
Employed persons			
Full-time workers, total	3,449	29,613	37,094
35 hours of more	2,990	25,427	31,774
at work 1 to 34 hours			
for economic reasons	80	421	559
not at work	122	1,161	1,454
Part-time workers, total	631	5,716	7,010
at work for economic reasons	175	696	996
not at work	29	435	516
Unemployed persons			
Looking for full-time work	270	1,238	1,991
Looking for part-time work	53	305	445
West			
Employed persons			
Full-time workers, total	4,311	19,096	22,373
35 hours of more	3,762	16,512	19,379
at work 1 to 34 hours			
for economic reasons	130	353	401
not at work	136	705	817
Part-time workers, total	858	4,673	5,361
at work for economic reasons	244	724	878
not at work	47	327	363
Unemployed persons			
Looking for full-time work	469	1,249	1,536
Looking for part-time work	88	314	384

SOURCE: U.S. Department of Labor, Bureau of Labor Statistics, Geographic Profile of Employment and Unemployment, 1996, pp. 10-11, table 2. L 2.3/12:996

NOTES: 'Total' includes other races and ethnic groups not shown separately. The full-time labor force includes persons working part time for economic reasons (slack work; material shortages; repairs to plant or equipment; start or termination of a job during the week; and inability to find full time work).

UNITS: Members of the civilian labor force in thousands of persons, by status, as shown.

Table 7.10 Unemployment Rates for the Civilian Labor Force, by Age, 1985, 1990, 1997

	Hispanic	White	Total
1985			
unemployment rate			
all ages	10.5%	6.2%	7.2%
- persons 16-19 years old	24.3	15.7	18.6
- persons 20 years old and over	9.4	5.5	6.4
- persons 65 years old and over	8.1	2.9	3.2
1990			
unemployment rate			
all ages	8.0%	4.7%	5.5%
- persons 16-19 years old	19.5	13.4	15.5
- persons 25 years old and over	6.8	3.8	4.4
- persons 55 years old and over	6.4	3.4	3.6
1997			
unemployment rate			
all ages	7.7%	4.2%	4.9%
- persons 16-19 years old	21.6	13.6	16.0
- persons 20-24 years old	10.3	6.9	8.5
- persons 25-54 years old	6.1	3.3	3.9
- persons 55-64 years old	6.5	2.7	2.9
- persons 65 years old and over	6.8	3.0	3.3

SOURCE: U.S. Department of Labor, Bureau of Labor Statistics, Handbook of Labor Statistics, 1989, pp. 136-141, table 28, (data from the Current Population Survey). L 2.3/5:989
U.S. Department of Labor, Bureau of Labor Statistics, *Employment and Earnings*, January, 1991, p. 208, table 39, p. 212, table 44; January, 1998, p. 164-165, table 3, p. 167, table 4 (data from the Current Population Survey). L 2.41/2:(vol)/1:(year)

NOTES: 'Total' includes other races and ethnic groups not shown separately.
Data covers members of the civilian labor force.

UNITS: Unemployment rate, by age group as shown.

Table 7.11 Unemployment Rates for the Civilian Labor Force, by Sex and Age, 1985, 1990, 1997

	Hispanic		White		Total	
	male	female	male	female	male	female
1985						
unemployment rate						
all ages	10.2	11.0%	6.1%	6.4%	7.0%	7.4%
- persons 16-19 years old	24.7	23.8	16.5	14.8	19.5	17.6
- persons 20 years old						
and over	9.1	9.9	5.4	5.7	6.2	6.6
- persons 65 years old						
and over	9.4	5.5	2.7	3.1	3.1	3.3
1990						
unemployment rate						
all ages	7.8%	8.3%	4.8%	4.6%	5.5%	5.6%
- persons 16-19 years old	19.4	19.6	14.2	12.6	16.3	14.7
- persons 20 years old						
and over	7.0	7.4	4.3	4.1	4.9	4.8
- persons 65 years old						
and over	na	na	2.8	2.8	3.0	3.1
1997						
unemployment rate						
all ages	7.0%	8.9%	4.2%	4.2%	4.9%	5.0%
- persons 16-19 years old	20.8	22.7	14.3	12.8	16.9	15.0
- persons 20-24 years old	9.8	11.0	7.3	6.4	8.9	8.1
- persons 25-54 years old	5.2	7.4	3.3	3.5	3.7	4.1
- persons 55-64 years old	6.8	6.1	2.9	2.4	3.1	2.7
- persons 65 years old						
and over	7.2	6.0	2.7	3.4	3.0	3.6

SOURCE: U.S. Department of Labor, Bureau of Labor Statistics, Handbook of Labor Statistics, 1989, pp. 136-141, table 28, (data from the Current Population Survey). L 2.3/5:989
U.S. Department of Labor, Bureau of Labor Statistics, *Employment and Earnings*, January, 1991, p. 208, table 39, p. 212, table 44; January, 1998, p. 164-165, table 3, p. 167, table 4 (data from the Current Population Survey). L 2.41/2:(vol)/1:(year)

NOTES: 'Total' includes other races and ethnic groups not shown separately.
Data covers members of the civilian labor force.

UNITS: Unemployment rate, by age group as shown.

Table 7.12   Unemployment Rates for the Hispanic Civilian Labor Force, by Sex, by Type of Hispanic Origin, 1985, 1990, 1997

	type of origin					
	Mex-ican	Puerto Rican	Cuban	Central/South Amer	other Hispanic	total Hispanic
1985						
Unemployment rate						
both sexes	11.9%	14.3%	6.8%	11.0%	7.1%	11.3%
males	12.5	15.0	6.9	9.3	8.9	11.8
females	10.9	13.3	6.6	13.2	4.9	10.5
1990						
Unemployment rate						
both sexes	9.0%	8.6%	5.8%	6.6%	6.2%	8.2%
males	8.6	8.2	6.3	6.9	6.2	8.0
females	9.8	9.1	5.1	6.3	5.9	8.5
1997						
Unemployment rate						
both sexes	9.5%	11.4%	6.1%	6.9%	11.5%	9.2%
males	9.1	14.3	6.4	6.7	11.0	9.2
females	10.2	8.1	5.6	7.0	12.0	9.3

SOURCE: U.S. Bureau of the Census, The Hispanic Population in the United States: March, 1985, pp. 14-15, table 2 (data from U.S. Bureau of the Census, *Current Population Reports*).   C 3.186:P-20/422
U.S. Bureau of the Census, The Hispanic Population in the United States:, March, 1990, pp. 8-9, table 2; March, 1992, pp. 14-15, table 2 (data from U.S. Bureau of the Census, *Current Population Reports*).   C 3.186/14-2:(year)
U.S. Census Bureau, "Hispanic Population of the United States, (Table 7.2). March, 1997 CPS: Employment Status of the Civilian Labor Force by Race - Ethnicity Age 16 and Over: by Sex - Value;", released 7 August 1998; < http://www.census.gov/population/socdemo/hispanic/cps97/tab07-2.txt >

NOTES: Total population includes other races and ethnic groups not shown separately. 'Other Hispanic origin' includes persons from Spain and persons identifying themselves generally as Hispanic, Spanish, Spanish-American, Hispano, Latino, etc.

UNITS: Total population in thousands of persons 16 years old and over; percent as a percent of total shown (100.0%).

Table 7.13 Unemployment by Reason for Unemployment, by Region, 1990, 1992 and 1996

	Hispanic	White	Total
1990			
Northeast			
job losers	56.7%	56.7%	55.7%
job leavers	9.9	12.1	12.3
reentrants to the labor force	22.0	23.3	23.7
new entrants to the labor force	11.4	7.8	8.2
Midwest			
job losers	54.2%	52.5%	50.7%
job leavers	9.4	14.7	13.8
reentrants to the labor force	27.3	25.6	26.8
new entrants to the labor force	9.0	7.2	8.8
South			
job losers	47.6%	44.0%	43.3%
job leavers	16.7	18.0	16.1
reentrants to the labor force	23.4	28.2	29.2
new entrants to the labor force	12.4	9.8	11.4
West			
job losers	55.5%	47.8%	46.7%
job leavers	12.5	16.2	16.0
reentrants to the labor force	20.0	27.9	28.7
new entrants to the labor force	12.1	8.1	8.5
1992			
Northeast			
job losers	65.5%	67.1%	65.9%
job leavers	6.9	7.0	6.8
reentrants to the labor force	16.5	18.8	19.3
new entrants to the labor force	11.1	7.1	8.0
Midwest			
job losers	57.6%	57.6%	55.3%
job leavers	8.7	11.7	11.0
reentrants to the labor force	23.2	22.1	23.6
new entrants to the labor force	10.6	8.7	10.1

continued on the next page

Table 7.13   continued

	Hispanic	White	Total
1992 - continued			
South			
job losers	55.3%	52.0%	50.4%
job leavers	10.8	13.2	12.1
reentrants to the labor force	23.1	26.3	27.1
new entrants to the labor force	10.8	8.5	10.3
West			
job losers	63.0%	58.4%	56.9%
job leavers	7.0	10.8	10.7
reentrants to the labor force	18.2	22.7	23.3
new entrants to the labor force	11.8	8.2	9.1
1996			
Northeast			
job losers	46.8%	55.0%	53.1%
job leavers	6.5	8.4	7.6
reentrants to the labor force	35.6·	30.4	32.4
new entrants to the labor force	11.3	6.4	7.2
Midwest			
job losers	46.3%	48.1%	45.7%
job leavers	9.3	12.4	11.4
reentrants to the labor force	34.1	33.9	36.5
new entrants to the labor force	10.3	5.6	6.3
South			
job losers	44.4%	45.0%	42.9%
job leavers	12.9	14.5	13.1
reentrants to the labor force	31.8	32.6	35.0
new entrants to the labor force	11.0	7.9	9.0
West			
job losers	51.6%	48.8%	47.5%
job leavers	5.6	9.6	9.5
reentrants to the labor force	31.6	34.0	34.7
new entrants to the labor force	11.4	8.1	8.8

SOURCE: U.S. Department of Labor, Bureau of Labor Statistics, <u>Geographic Profile of Employment and Unemployment</u>, <u>1990</u>, pp. 29-30, table 10; <u>1992</u>, pp. 31-32, table 10; <u>1996</u>, pp. 31-32, table 10. L 2.3/12:(year)

NOTES: 'Total' includes other races and ethnic groups not shown separately. Data covers members of the civilian labor force.

UNITS: Unemployed members of the civilian labor force in thousands of persons, by reason for unemployment as shown.

Table 7.14 Duration of Unemployment, by Region of Residence, 1992 and 1996

	Hispanic	White	Total
1992			
Northeast			
less than 5 weeks	26.6%	25.9%	25.5%
5-14 weeks	28.0	27.9	27.8
15 weeks and over	45.4	46.1	46.7
27 weeks and over	26.0	28.0	28.5
52 weeks and over	15.1	14.5	15.5
Midwest			
less than 5 weeks	36.9%	36.2%	37.0%
5-14 weeks	32.4	30.4	30.5
15 weeks and over	30.7	33.4	32.5
27 weeks and over	16.8	18.5	18.2
52 weeks and over	8.8	10.0	10.2
South			
less than 5 weeks	43.6%	38.7%	38.0%
5-14 weeks	27.9	29.7	29.6
15 weeks and over	28.5	31.7	32.4
27 weeks and over	15.4	18.1	18.4
52 weeks and over	6.8	9.4	10.1
West			
less than 5 weeks	40.3%	38.3%	37.3%
5-14 weeks	28.4	29.0	29.7
15 weeks and over	31.3	32.7	33.0
27 weeks and over	17.2	18.1	18.4
52 weeks and over	9.5	9.4	9.6
1996			
Northeast			
less than 5 weeks	30.7%	33.1%	30.8%
5-14 weeks	30.9	31.9	30.9
15 weeks and over	36.5	35.2	36.4
27 weeks and over	23.4	19.2	22.2
52 weeks and over	14.6	10.8	13.1

continued on the next page

Table 7.14   continued

	Hispanic	White	Total
1996 - continued			
Midwest			
less than 5 weeks	37.7%	41.3%	39.1%
5-14 weeks	32.6	32.8	32.7
15 weeks and over	29.6	25.9	28.1
27 weeks and over	15.5	12.1	13.7
52 weeks and over	8.5	6.5	7.6
South			
less than 5 weeks	38.8%	41.3%	38.5%
5-14 weeks	30.7	31.3	32.3
15 weeks and over	30.6	27.4	29.3
27 weeks and over	16.1	14.0	15.5
52 weeks and over	7.6	6.5	7.6
West			
less than 5 weeks	35.6%	37.5%	36.2%
5-14 weeks	29.7	30.1	30.4
15 weeks and over	35.2	33.0	34.0
27 weeks and over	20.2	18.8	19.4
52 weeks and over	11.5	10.4	10.9

SOURCE: U.S. Department of Labor, Bureau of Labor Statistics, <u>Geographic Profile of Employment and Unemployment</u>, <u>1992</u>, pp. 33-34, table 11, <u>1996</u>, pp. 33-34, table 11. L 2.3/12:(year)

NOTES: 'Total' includes other races and ethnic groups not shown separately.

UNITS: Duration of unemployment by region as a percent of total unemployment in each region, 100.0%.

Table 7.15 Workers Paid Hourly Rates With Earnings at or Below the Minimum Wage, 1997

	Hispanic	White	Total
Number of workers			
All workers paid hourly rates	8,765	58,395	71,081
at or below $4.75 per hour	984	4,863	6,237
at $4.75 per hour	388	1,632	2,115
below $4.75 per hour	596	3,231	4,122
Percent of all workers paid hourly rates			
All at or below $4.75 per hour	11.2%	8.3%	8.8%
at $4.75 per hour	4.4	2.8	3.0
below $4.75 per hour	6.8	5.5	5.8
Median hourly earnings	$7.61	$8.97	$8.84

SOURCE: U.S. Bureau of the Census, <u>Statistical Abstract of the United States, 1998</u>, p. 438, table 700 (data from the U.S. Bureau of Labor Statistics). C 3.134:998

NOTES: 'Total' includes other races/ethnic groups not shown separately. Workers 16 years and over.

UNITS: Number of workers in thousands; 'percent of all workers paid hourly rates' in percent, as a percent of total, 100.0%; median hourly earnings of workers paid hourly rates in dollars per hour.

Table 7.16　　　Union Membership, by Sex, 1997

	Hispanic	White	Total
Men			
total employed	7,153	50,941	59,825
members of unions number	904	8,171	9,763
as a percent of total employed	12.6%	16.0%	16.3%
represented by unions total	1,023	8,859	10,619
as a percent of total employed	14.3%	17.4%	17.7%
Women			
total employed	4,728	45,163	54,708
members of unions number	503	4,917	6,347
as a percent of total employed	10.6%	10.9%	11.6%
represented by unions total	579	5,679	7,304
as a percent of total employed	12.2%	12.6%	13.4%

SOURCE:　U.S. Department of Labor, Bureau of Labor Statistics, *Employment and Earnings*, January 1998, p. 215, table 40, (data from the Current Population Survey). L 2.41/2:40/1:998

NOTES:　'Total' includes other races/ethnic groups not shown separately. 'Members of unions' includes members of a labor union or an employee association similar to a union. 'Represented by unions' includes members of a labor union or an employee association similar to a union as well as workers who report no union affiliation but whose jobs are covered by a union or an employee association contract.

UNITS:　Total employed, members of unions and represented by unions in thousands of persons 16 years old and older; percent as shown.

Table 7.17 Educational Attainment of Persons 16 Years and Over, by Labor Force Status and Sex, 1997

	Hispanic		White		Total	
	male	female	male	female	male	female
High school graduate or more						
In civilian labor force	55.7%	68.0%	84.1%	88.7%	83.8%	88.1%
Employed	57.0	69.8	85.2	89.6	85.0	89.2
Unemployed	42.8	50.2	63.9	66.4	64.3	68.5
Not in labor force	32.1	34.6	61.9	67.5	59.5	65.5
Bachelor's degree or more						
In civilian labor force	9.5%	11.6%	26.4%	25.7%	25.8%	24.7%
Employed	10.1	12.4	27.4	26.4	26.8	25.6
Unemployed	3.1	3.5	9.7	10.4	9.3	9.7
Not in labor force	3.8	4.3	14.2	11.8	13.0	11.4

SOURCE: U.S. Bureau of the Census, <u>Current Population Reports: Educational Attainment in the United States: March 1997</u>, Series P-20, #505, pp. 35-38, table 6. <www.census.gov/prod/3/98pubs/p20-505u.pdf>, accessed 15 October 1998.

NOTES: 'Total' includes other races and ethnic groups not shown separately.

UNITS: Percent distribution as a percent of total, 100.0%.

Table 7.18 Unemployment Rates of the Civilian Labor Force 25 - 64 Years of Age, by Educational Attainment, 1992 - 1997

	Hispanic	White	Total
1992			
Total	9.8%	6.0%	6.7%
less than a high school diploma	13.6	12.9	13.5
high school graduate, no college	9.6	6.8	7.7
less than a bachelor's degree	5.9	5.3	5.9
college graduate	4.2	2.7	2.9
1993			
Total	10.3%	5.8%	6.4%
less than a high school diploma	14.5	12.4	13.0
high school graduate, no college	9.1	6.5	7.3
less than a bachelor's degree	7.0	5.0	5.5
college graduate	5.2	3.1	3.2
1994			
Total	9.7%	5.2%	5.8%
less than a high school diploma	13.4	11.7	12.6
high school graduate, no college	8.3	5.8	6.7
less than a bachelor's degree	7.2	4.5	5.0
college graduate	5.2	2.6	2.9
1997			
Total	7.3%	3.9%	4.4%
less than a high school diploma	9.6	9.4	10.4
high school graduate, no college	7.5	4.6	5.1
less than a bachelor's degree	5.5	3.4	3.8
college graduate	3.0	1.8	2.0

SOURCE: U.S. Bureau of the Census, <u>Statistical Abstract of the United States,</u> <u>1998</u>, p. 422, table 681 (data from U.S. Department of Labor, Bureau of Labor Statistics). C 3.134:98

NOTES: 'Total' includes other races/ethnic groups not shown separately. Data is for persons 25 years old and over.

UNITS: Unemployment rates (percent of the civilian labor force that is unemployed) as a percent of the total civilian labor force.

Table 7.19 Self-employed Persons, 1997

	Hispanic	White	Total
1997			
worked at home	156	3,868	4,125
percent who worked less than 8 hours	27.8%	30.5%	30.4%
8 hours or more			
total	72.2	69.5	69.6
35 hours or more	31.3	29.0	29.3
mean hours:			
worked at home	23.8	22.9	23.0
total at work on primary job	35.9	36.9	37.3

SOURCE: U.S. Department of Labor, Bureau of Labor Statistics, "Table 5: Home-based businesses: Self-employed persons by selected characteristics, May 1997;" pp. 1-2, table 5. <http://stats.bls.gov/news.release/homey.t05.htm> accesses 19 November, 1998.

NOTES: Data refer to employed persons in nonagricultural industries who reported work in a home-based business during the survey reference week as part of their primary job. Detail for the above race and Hispanic-origin groups will not sum to totals because data for the "other races" group are not presented and Hispanics are included in both the white and black population groups. Data reflect revised population controls used in the Current Population Survey effective with January 1997 estimates.

UNITS: Numbers in thousands of persons. Percent as a percent of persons working at home.

Table 7.20 Unemployment, by Reason for Unemployment, 1994 - 1997

	Hispanic	White	Total
1994			
Total	1,187	5,892	7,996
job losers	573	2,972	3,815
job leavers	89	638	791
reentrants to the labor force	402	1,898	2,786
new entrants to the labor force	124	385	604
1997			
Total	1,069	4,836	6,739
job losers	500	2,284	3,037
job leavers	96	623	795
reentrants to the labor force	350	1,576	2,338
new entrants to the labor force	122	354	569

SOURCE: U.S. Department of Labor, Bureau of Labor Statistics, *Employment and Earnings*, January, 1996, p. 196, table 28; January, 1998, p. 200, table 28 (data from the Current Population Survey). L2.41/2:(vol)/1:(year)

NOTES: 'Total' includes other races and ethnic groups not shown separately. Data covers members of the civilian labor force.

UNITS: Unemployed members of the civilian labor force in thousands of persons, by reason for unemployment as shown.

Table 7.21   Self-Employed Workers, 1994 - 1997

	Hispanic	White	Total
1994	533	8,179	9,003
1995	507	8,105	8,902
1996	561	8,106	8,971
1997	598	8,153	9,056

SOURCE: U.S. Department of Labor, Bureau of Labor Statistics, *Employment and Earnings*, January, 1994, p. 230, table 41; January, 1998, p. 180, table 12 (data from the Current Population Survey). L2.41/2:(vol)/1:(year)

NOTES: 'Total' includes other races and ethnic groups not shown separately.

UNITS: Self-employed workers in thousands of persons.

Table 7.22 Employment Status of Families, 1997

	Hispanic	White	All Races
Total families	6,779	58,514	69,714
With employed member(s)	5,701	48,378	57,289
Some usually work full time	5,285	45,069	53,226
With no employed member	1,078	10,135	12,425
With unemployed member(s)	789	3,566	4,913
Some member(s) employed	532	2,632	3,445
Some usually work full time	473	2,353	3,070

SOURCE: U.S. Department Labor, Bureau Labor Statistics; "Employment Characteristics of Families, 1997 (Table) 1. Employment and unemployment in families, by race and Hispanic origin, 1996-97 annual averages"; (accessed: 19 November 1998); <http://stats.bls.gov/news.release/famee.t01.htm>

NOTES: 'Total' includes other races and ethnic groups not shown separately.

UNITS: Number of families in thousands of families.

Chapter 8: Earnings, Income, Poverty & Wealth

Table 8.01 Money Income of Households, 1980 - 1997

	Hispanic	White	Total
Median income			
1980	$24,582	$33,645	$31,891
1985	24,055	34,306	32,530
1986	24,815	35,394	33,665
1987	25,225	35,821	33,999
1988	25,505	36,055	34,106
1989	26,199	36,340	34,547
1990	25,320	35,413	33,952
1991	24,690	34,350	32,780
1992	23,869	34,023	32,361
1993	23,472	33,804	32,041
1994	23,421	34,028	32,264
1996	24,906	37,161	35,492
1997	26,628	38,972	37,005
Mean income			
1980	$30,025	$39,459	$37,929
1985	30,057	41,676	40,033
1986	31,334	43,324	41,592
1987	32,335	44,088	42,281
1988	32,563	44,432	42,615
1989	33,455	45,465	43,647
1990	31,717	44,122	42,411
1991	31,416	43,005	41,263
1992	30,445	42,880	41,027
1993	31,067	44,393	42,489
1994	31,582	45,034	43,133
1996	34,005	48,994	47,123
1997	35,883	51,902	49,692

SOURCE: U.S. Bureau of the Census, Current Population Reports: Income, Poverty, and Valuation of Noncash Benefits: 1994, Series P-60, #189, pp. B-2 - B-3, table B-1. C3.186/2:994
U.S. Bureau of the Census, Current Population Reports: Money Income in the United States: 1996, Series P-60, #197, p. 5, table 2 C3.186/2:996; 1997, Series P-60, #200, p. 5, table 2 <www.census.gov/prod/3/98pubs/p60-200.pdr> accessed 15 October 1998.

NOTES: 'Total' includes other races and ethnic groups not shown separately.

UNITS: Median and mean money income in 1994 CPI-U-XI adjusted dollars, as shown.

Table 8.02 Money Income of Households, by Selected Household
Characteristic, 1997

	Hispanic	White	Total
1997			
Number of households	8,590	86,106	102,528
number of households with			
current dollar incomes of:			
under $5,000	473	2,415	3,531
$5,000-$9,999	968	5,773	7,765
10,000-$14,999	916	6,716	8,326
$15,000-$24,999	1,691	12,549	15,244
$25,000-$34,999	1,290	11,350	13,586
$35,000-$49,999	1,429	14,170	16,698
$50,000-$74,999	1,047	16,190	18,531
$75,000-$99,999	427	8,183	9,186
$100,000 and over	351	8,762	9,661
median income	$26,628	$38,972	$37,005
mean income	$35,883	$51,902	$49,692
Median income by:			
type of residence			
inside metropolitan area	$27,078	$41,576	$39,381
outside metropolitan area	22,383	31,110	30,057
type of household			
family households	$29,253	$47,454	$45,347
married couple families	34,317	52,199	51,681
non-family households	16,807	22,380	21,705
male householder living alone	21,059	30,009	27,592
female householder living alone	11,485	17,997	17,613
age of householder			
15-24 years old	$19,341	$24,423	$22,583
25-34 years old	27,519	40,477	38,174
35-44 years old	31,148	49,695	46,359
45-54 years old	32,074	54,879	51,875
55-64 years old	27,648	43,052	41,356
65 years old and over	14,168	21,374	20,761

continued on the next page

Table 8.02 continued

	Hispanic	White	Total
1997 - continued			
size of household			
one person	$12,222	$19,288	$18,762
two persons	26,390	40,954	39,343
three persons	26,396	50,269	47,115
four persons	33,053	55,819	53,165
five persons	31,586	52,493	50,407
six persons	30,185	48,974	46,465
seven or more persons	36,088	46,044	42,343
number of earners			
no earners	$ 7,842	$15,324	$14,142
one earner	20,464	31,412	29,780
two earners or more	41,081	58,947	57,525
work experience of the householder			
all civilian householders	$26,628	$38,972	37,005
worked	32,019	47,973	45,877
worked year-round full-time	36,701	53,045	51,336
did not work	11,893	19,342	18,143
housing tenure			
owner occupied	$37,889	$46,578	$45,821
renter occupied	20,439	25,954	24,514

SOURCE: U.S. Bureau of the Census, <u>Current Population Reports: Money Income in the United States: 1997</u>, Series P-60, #200, pp. 1-4, table 1, p. 5, table 2. <www.census.gov/prod/3/98pubs/p60-200.pdf> accessed s15 October 1998.

NOTES: 'Total' includes other races and ethnic groups not shown separately. Number of households as of March of the <u>following</u> year. 'Occupation of the householder' represents the longest job held by the householder.

UNITS: Number of households in thousands; mean and median income in current dollars.

Table 8.03 Money Income of Households by Type of Hispanic Origin, 1991, 1997

	Mexican	Puerto Rican	Cuban	Central/ South Amer	other Hispanic	total Hispanic
1991						
All households	100.0%	100.0%	100.0%	100.0%	100.0%	100.0%
percent with incomes of:						
less than $10,000.	18.9	33.4	20.4	17.9	18.5	20.7
$10,000. to $24,999.	36.4	28.5	26.7	33.7	27.9	33.7
$25,000. to $49,999.	31.6	21.7	29.3	32.5	34.7	30.6
$50,000 or more	13.1	16.5	23.6	15.9	18.8	15.0
median income	$22,477	$17,967	$26,593	$24,157	$27,110	$22,688
mean income	$27,617	$25,736	$35,599	$30,824	$34,149	$28,872
1997						
All households	100.0%	100.0%	100.0%	100.0%	100.0%	100.0%
percent with incomes of:						
less than $10,000.	15.2	27.8	17.6	13.1	21.7	17.2
$10,000. to $24,999.	35.9	27.2	28.0	30.1	29.4	33.0
$25,000. to $49,999.	30.6	27.9	25.3	32.6	27.5	29.9
$50,000 or more	18.3	17.1	29.1	24.2	21.4	19.9

SOURCE: U.S. Bureau of the Census, The Hispanic Population in the United States: March, 1992, pp. 18-19, table 3; March , 1993, pp. 16-17, table 3 (data from U.S. Bureau of the Census, *Current Population Reports*). C 3.186/14-2:(year)
U.S. Bureau of the Census, "Hispanic Population of the US. (Table 6.9) March, 1997 CPS: Household Income by Race-Ethnicity (Collapsed Categories)-Values/Percents". Released 7 August 1998
http://www.census.gov/population/socdemo/hispanic/cps97/tab06-9.txt.

NOTES: Total population includes other races and ethnic groups not shown separately. 'Other Hispanic origin' includes persons from Spain and persons identifying themselves generally as Hispanic, Spanish, Spanish-American, Hispano, Latino, etc.

UNITS: Percent as a percent of total shown (100.0%), median income and mean income in current dollars.

Table 8.04   Money Income of Families, 1980 - 1997

	Hispanic	White	Total
Median income			
1980	$28,699	$42,717	$40,999
1985	28,381	43,484	41,371
1986	29,281	45,117	43,139
1987	28,681	45,755	43,756
1988	29,534	46,013	43,674
1989	30,347	46,564	44,284
1990	28,773	45,332	43,414
1991	28,158	44,524	42,351
1992	26,946	44,238	41,839
1993	26,273	43,652	41,051
1994	26,336	44,277	42,001
1995	25,876	44,913	42,769
1996	26,780	45,783	43,271
1997	28,142	46,754	44,568
Mean income			
1980	$34,352	$48,636	$45,754
1985	34,534	51,275	49,140
1986	35,789	53,328	51,143
1987	36,522	54,436	52,112
1988	37,074	54,692	52,380
1989	37,791	56,179	53,723
1990	35,994	54,685	52,377
1991	35,350	53,352	50,951
1992	34,292	53,118	50,588
1993	34,554	55,055	52,450
1994	35,034	56,001	53,435
1995	34,390	56,445	54,082
1996	36,409	57,486	54,908
1997	37,783	59,587	56,902

SOURCE: U.S. Bureau of the Census, <u>Current Population Reports: Money Income in the United States: 1997</u>, Series P-60, #200, pp. B-8 - B-9, table B-4. <www.census.gov/prod/3/98pubs/p60-200.pdf>, accessed 15 October 1998.

NOTES: 'Total' includes other races and ethnic groups not shown separately.

UNITS: Median and mean money income in 1997 CPI-U-XI adjusted dollars, as shown.

Table 8.05 Money Income of Families, by Selected Family Characteristic, 1985

	Hispanic	White	Total
Families			
Number of families	4,206	54,991	63,558
percent of families with incomes:			
under $2,500	2.9%	1.6%	1.9%
$2,500-$4,499	5.4	2.1	2.9
$5,000-$7,499	8.5	3.6	4.2
$7,500-$9,999	8.5	3.9	4.3
$10,000-$12,499	8.1	4.8	5.2
$12,500-$14,999	6.8	4.9	5.0
$15,000-$19,999	12.1	10.3	10.5
$20,000-$24,999	11.3	10.4	10.3
$25,000-$34,999	16.0	19.2	18.6
$35,000-$49,999	12.5	19.7	18.8
$50,000 and over	8.1	19.6	18.3
median income	$19,027	$29,152	$27,735
mean income	$23,152	$34,375	$32,944
Median family income by:			
type of family			
married couple families	$22,269	$31,602	$31,100
wife in paid labor force	28,132	36,992	36,431
wife not in paid labor force	17,116	25,307	24,556
male householder,			
no wife present	19,773	24,190	22,622
female householder,			
no husband present	8,792	15,825	13,660

continued on the next page

Table 8.05 continued

Mean family income by:	Hispanic	White	Total
type of income			
wages and salaries	$22,566	$31,277	$30,258
non-farm self-employment	14,628	14,565	14,420
farm self employment	na	4,593	4,557
property income	1,483	3,486	3,327
- interest income	1,017	2,440	2,328
transfer payments and all other income	5,347	7,776	7,469
- social security or railroad retirement income	6,014	7,684	7,488
-public assistance and supplemental income	4,458	3,416	3,498

SOURCE: U.S. Bureau of the Census, <u>Current Population Reports: Money Income of Households Families and Persons in the United States; March 1985</u>, Series P-60, #156, pp. 26-29, tables 9, 10; pp. 40-46, tables 13, 14; pp. 56-64, table 17; pp. 86-88, table 25. C3.186:P-60/156
U.S. Bureau of the Census, <u>Statistical Abstract of the United States, 1987</u>, p. 437, table 734, (data from *the Current Population Survey*). C 3.134:987

NOTES: 'Total' includes other races and ethnic groups not shown separately. Number of families as of March of the <u>following</u> year. 'Occupation of the householder' represents the longest job held by the householder. 'Property income' includes interest, dividends, net rental income, income from trusts and estates, and net royalty income.

UNITS: Number of families and families with income, in thousands of families; percent as a percent as shown; mean income in current dollars.

Table 8.06 Money Income of Families, by Selected Family Characteristic, 1990

	Hispanic	White	Total
Families			
Number of families	4,981	58,803	66,322
percent of families with current dollar incomes of:			
under $5,000	6.3%	2.5%	3.6%
$5,000-$9,999	12.3	4.7	5.8
$10,000-$14,999	12.6	7.0	7.5
$15,000-$24,999	21.7	16.0	16.4
$25,000-$34,999	16.6	16.5	16.2
$35,000-$49,999	15.7	20.8	20.0
$50,000-$74,999	10.0	19.3	18.2
$75,000-$99,999	2.9	7.3	6.9
$100,000 and over	1.9	5.9	5.4
mean income	$29,311	$44,532	$42,652
median income	$23,341	$36,915	$35,353
Median income by:			
type of residence			
nonfarm	$23,402	$36,974	$35,376
farm	na	34,476	34,171
inside metropolitan area	23,898	40,086	37,893
outside metropolitan area	19,061	29,693	28,272
type of family			
married couple families	$27,996	$40,331	$39,895
wife in paid labor force	34,778	47,247	46,777
wife not in paid labor force	21,168	30,781	30,265
male householder, no wife present	21,744	30,570	29,046
female householder, no husband present	11,914	19,528	16,932

continued on the next page

Table 8.06 continued

	Hispanic	White	Total
Median income by:			
age of householder			
15-24 years old	$13,009	$18,234	$16,219
25-34 years old	20,439	33,457	31,497
35-44 years old	27,350	42,632	41,061
45-54 years old	29,908	49,249	47,165
55-64 years old	30,839	40,416	39,035
65 years old and over	17,962	25,864	25,049
size of family			
two persons	$19,230	$31,734	$30,428
three persons	22,778	38,858	36,644
four persons	25,808	43,352	41,451
five persons	25,727	41,037	39,452
six persons	24,786	40,387	38,379
seven or more persons	30,549	39,845	35,363
number of earners			
no earners	$ 8,858	$17,369	$15,047
one earner	16,795	27,670	25,878
two earners or more	33,704	46,261	45,462

SOURCE: U.S. Bureau of the Census, <u>Current Population Reports: Money Income of Households, Families, and Persons in the United States: March 1990</u>, Series P-60, #174, pp. 52-55, table 13; p. 56, table 14. C3.186/2:990

NOTES: 'Total' includes other races and ethnic groups not shown separately. Number of families as of March of the following year.

UNITS: Number of families and families with income, in thousands of families; percent as a percent as shown; mean and median income in current dollars.

Table 8.07 Money Income of Families, by Selected Family Characteristic, 1997

	Hispanic	White	Total
Families			
Number of families	6,961	59,515	70,884
with current dollar incomes of:			
under $5,000	352	1,262	1,929
$5,000-$9,999	604	1,923	2,887
$10,000-$14,999	759	3,047	4,054
$15,000-$24,999	1,397	7,454	9,250
$25,000-$34,999	1,066	7,552	9,079
$35,000-$49,999	1,199	10,527	12,357
$50,000-$74,999	887	13,172	15,112
$75,000-$99,999	379	6,973	7,826
$100,000 and over	318	7,605	8,391
median income	$28,142	$46,754	$44,568
mean income	$37,783	$59,587	$56,902
Median income by:			
type of residence			
inside metropolitan area	$28,708	$50,410	$47,315
outside metropolitan area	24,130	37,305	36,149
type of family			
married couple families	$33,914	$52,098	$51,591
wife in paid labor force	42,280	61,441	60,669
wife not in paid labor force	23,749	36,343	36,027
male householder, no wife present	25,543	34,802	32,960
female householder,			
no husband present	14,994	22,999	21,023

continued on the next page

Table 8.07 continued

	Hispanic	White	Total
Median income by:			
age of householder			
15-24 years old	$17,899	$22,431	$20,820
25-34 years old	26,291	41,890	39,979
35-44 years old	31,431	52,753	50,424
45-54 years old	34,592	61,852	59,959
55-64 years old	33,628	51,598	50,241
65 years old and over	22,677	31,167	30,660
size of family			
two persons	$23,593	$39,492	$37,562
three persons	26,210	50,149	46,783
four persons	31,462	56,022	53,350
five persons	31,175	53,696	51,101
six persons	30,233	48,079	45,473
seven or more persons	35,508	45,816	42,001
number of earners			
no earners	$ 8,870	$21,516	$19,731
one earner	19,662	32,811	30,204
two earners or more	41,153	60,291	58,972

SOURCE: U.S. Bureau of the Census, <u>Current Population Reports: Money Income in the United States: 1997</u>, Series P-60, #200, pp. 13-16, table 4; p. 17, table 5. <www.census.gov/prod/3/98pubs/p60-200.pdf>, accessed 15 October 1998.

NOTES: 'Total' includes other races and ethnic groups not shown separately. Number of families as of March of the <u>following</u> year.

UNITS: Number of families and families with income, in thousands of families; mean and median income in current dollars.

Table 8.08 Money Income of Families, by Type of Hispanic Origin, 1991, 1997

		type of origin				
	Mexican	Puerto Rican	Cuban	Central/ South Amer	other Hispanic	total Hispanic
1991						
All families	100.0%	100.0%	100.0%	100.0%	100.0%	100.0%
percent with incomes of:						
less than $10,000.	18.0	29.2	13.4	17.0	16.2	18.8
$10,000. to $24,999.	36.7	27.3	25.4	33.1	25.0	33.5
$25,000. to $49,999.	31.8	25.2	32.9	32.2	36.2	31.5
$50,000 or more	13.5	18.3	28.3	17.7	22.6	16.2
median income	$23,018	$20,654	$30,095	$24,999	$30,155	$23,884
mean income	$27,968	$27,908	$40,030	$32,228	$37,697	$29,998
1997						
All families	100.0%	100.0%	100.0%	100.0%	100.0%	100.0%
percent with incomes of:						
less than $10,000.	13.6	24.1	10.2	10.4	20.0	14.6
$10,000. to $24,999.	35.8	28.1	25.5	31.3	28.2	33.1
$25,000. to $49,999.	31.3	29.1	29.1	32.3	27.8	30.8
$50,000 or more	19.4	18.7	35.3	26.1	23.9	21.5

SOURCE: U.S. Bureau of the Census, The Hispanic Population in the United States: March, 1991, pp. 20-21, table 4; (data from U.S. Bureau of the Census, *Current Population Reports*). C 3.186/14-2:991
U.S. Bureau of the Census, "Hispanic Population of the US (Table 4.8) March 1997 CPS: Family Income in Previous Year by Race-Ethnicity (Collapsed Categories)-Values/Percents". Released 7 August 1998. http://www.census.gov/population/socdemo/hispanic/cps97/tab04-8.txt.

NOTES: 'Other Hispanic origin' includes persons from Spain and persons identifying themselves generally as Hispanic, Spanish, Spanish-American, Hispano, Latino, etc. Income from the previous year.

UNITS: Percent as a percent of total shown (100.0%), median income and a mean income in current dollars.

Table 8.09 Median Weekly Earnings of Families, by Type of Family and Number of Earners, 1985, 1990, 1993

	Hispanic	White	Total
1985			
All families with earners	na	$543	$522
married couple families	na	589	582
with one earner	na	395	385
with two or more earners	na	723	715
families maintained by women	na	311	297
families maintained by men	na	475	450
1990			
All families with earners	$496	$681	$653
married couple families	555	745	732
with one earner	322	473	455
with two or more earners	716	892	880
families maintained by women	326	382	363
families maintained by men	468	539	514
1993			
All families with earners	$505	$739	$707
married couple families	566	816	804
with one earner	334	492	481
with two or more earners	744	984	973
families maintained by women	353	415	393
families maintained by men	432	547	523

SOURCE: U.S. Department of Labor, Bureau of Labor Statistics, <u>Handbook of Labor Statistics, 1989</u>, p. 200, table 44 (data from the Current Population Survey). L 2.3/5:989
U.S. Department of Labor, Bureau of Labor Statistics, *Employment and Earnings*, January, 1991, p. 219, table 52; January, 1994, p. 239, table 52 (data from the Current Population Survey). L 2.41/2:37/1:(year)

NOTES: 'Total' includes other races and ethnic groups not shown separately. Data excludes families in which there is no wage or salary earner, or in which the husband, wife, or other person maintaining the family is either self-employed or in the armed forces.

UNITS: Median weekly earnings in dollars.

Table 8.10 Median Income of Year-Round, Full-Time Workers, by Sex, 1980 - 1997

	Hispanic		White		Total	
	male	female	male	female	male	female
1980	$23,113	$16,500	$32,658	$19,224	$31,729	$19,088
1981	22,921	16,707	32,243	18,854	31,548	18,687
1982	22,574	16,308	31,703	19,313	30,932	19,099
1983	22,776	16,430	31,577	19,814	30,822	19,601
1984	22,875	16,940	32,357	20,125	31,352	19,958
1985	22,233	17,037	32,678	20,596	31,548	20,372
1986	21,525	17,712	33,189	21,022	32,330	20,779
1987	21,532	17,939	32,764	21,088	32,044	20,886
1988	21,171	17,606	32,292	21,133	31,613	20,880
1989	20,771	17,721	32,293	21,409	30,924	21,236
1990	20,542	16,823	31,002	21,521	29,711	21,278
1991	20,366	16,733	31,177	21,420	30,307	21,172
1992	20,049	17,138	31,012	21,659	30,358	21,440
1993	20,423	17,112	31,832	22,979	31,077	22,469
1994	20,525	18,418	32,440	23,894	31,612	23,265
1995	20,553	17,855	33,515	24,264	32,199	23,777
1996	21,265	19,272	34,741	25,358	33,538	24,935
1997	21,799	19,676	36,118	26,470	35,248	26,029

SOURCE: U.S. Bureau of the Census, Current Population Reports: Money Income of Households, Families, and Persons in the United States: March 1992, Series P-60, #184, p. B 36, table B-17; 1996, Series P-60, #197, pp.28-29, table 7. C3.186/2:(year)

U.S. Bureau of the Census, Current Population Reports: Income Poverty, and Valuation of Noncash Benefits: 1994, Series P-60, #189, pp. 15-16, table 5. C3.186/2:994

U.S. Bureau of the Census, Current Population Reports: Money Income in the United States: 1997, Series P-60, #200, pp. 28-29, table 7. <www.census.gov/prod/3/98pubs/p60-200.pdf>, accessed 15 October 1998.

NOTES: 'Total' includes other races/ethnic groups not shown separately. Data covers the earnings of wage and salary workers who usually worked 35 or more hours per week for 50 to 52 weeks during the year. Data prior to 1989 are for civilian workers only.

UNITS: Median money earnings.

Table 8.11 Money Income of Persons 15 Years Old and Older, by Selected Characteristic, 1985

	Hispanic		White		Total	
	male	female	male	female	male	female
Number of persons	6,232	6,366	76,617	82,345	88,474	96,354
persons with incomes:						
under $2,000	444	957	5,180	14,024	6,304	15,848
$2,000-$2,999	199	370	1,808	4,420	2,297	5,425
$3,000-$3,999	264	371	2,190	4,856	2,671	5,958
$4,000-$4,999	203	390	2,095	4,635	2,642	5,693
$5,000-$5,999	368	328	2,169	4,201	2,595	4,848
$6,000-$6,999	301	311	2,278	3,992	2,708	4,648
$7,000-$8,499	416	406	3,402	5,006	4,132	5,855
$8,500-$9,999	325	228	2,896	3,779	3,353	4,288
$10,000-$12,499	599	422	5,895	6,579	6,859	7,576
$12,500-$14,999	392	241	4,527	4,672	5,245	5,339
$15,000-$17,499	431	241	4,940	4,359	5,739	5,012
$17,500-$19,999	281	175	3,869	2,980	4,423	3,432
$20,000-$24,999	468	206	7,521	4,839	8,410	5,513
$25,000-$29,999	349	98	6,374	2,759	7,018	3,194
$30,000-$34,999	221	59	5,324	1,437	5,767	1,633
$35,000-$49,999	267	29	7,730	1,450	8,211	1,585
$50,000-$74,999	71	8	3,421	484	3,588	509
$75,000 and over	224	4	1,603	169	1,669	177
median income	$11,434	$ 6,020	$17,111	$ 7,357	$16,311	$ 7,217
mean income	$14,490	$ 8,178	$21,523	$10,317	$20,652	$10,173

Mean income by:

occupation

managerial, professional specialty	$27,148	$17,471	$34,711	$17,763	$34,201	$17,857
technical, sales, administrative support	17,692	10,461	24,050	10,988	23,293	11,076
service occupations	11,712	5,879	13,161	5,935	12,549	6,104
farming, forestry, fishing	7,451	na	8,241	3,865	8,024	3,762

continued on the next page

Table 8.11 continued

	Hispanic		White		Total	
	male	**female**	**male**	**female**	**male**	**female**
Mean income by:						
occupation - continued						
precision production,						
craft, repair	$16,015	$11,217	$20,593	$12,998	$20,277	$12,595
operators, fabricators,						
laborers	13,289	9,649	16,378	9,528	15,971	$9,548
work experience						
worked at full time jobs	$16,297	$11,616	$24,531	$14,556	$23,767	$14,364
worked 50-52 weeks	19,666	14,576	28,140	17,249	27,414	17,028
type of income						
wages and salaries	$14,689	$ 9,557	$21,848	$11,295	$21,056	$11,239
non-farm self-employment	14,026	7,818	16,083	5,885	15,834	5,867
farm self employment	na	na	4,234	1,654	4,184	1,695
property income	877	866	1,866	2,021	1,794	1,937
- interest income	541	605	1,305	1,454	1,254	1,395
transfer payments and all						
other income	4,313	3,686	6,812	4,428	6,572	4,318
- social security or						
railroad retirement	4,793	3,733	5,803	4,330	5,701	4,261
-public assistance and						
supplemental income	3,010	3,696	2,526	2,881	2,560	2,919

SOURCE: U.S. Bureau of the Census, Current Population Reports: Money Income of Households in the United States; March 1985, Series P-60, #156, pp. 107-109, table 31; pp. 135-138, table 35; pp. 141-143, table 37; pp. 160-163, tables 40, 41. C3.186:P-60/156

NOTES: 'Total' includes other races and ethnic groups not shown separately. Number of persons as of March of the following year. Data is based on persons living in households. Persons with incomes under $2,000 includes those with a loss. Occupation represents the longest job held by the person during the year. Educational attainment covers persons 25 years old and older; income covers persons 15 years old and older. 'Property income' includes interest, dividends, net rental income, income from trusts and estates, and net royalty income.

UNITS: Number of persons and persons by income in thousands of persons; median and mean income in dollars.

Table 8.12 Money Income of Persons 15 Years Old and Older, by Selected Characteristic, 1990

	Hispanic		White		Total	
	male	female	male	female	male	female
Number of persons	7,502	7,559	79,555	85,012	92,240	100,680
persons with incomes:						
under $5,000	1,053	2,059	8,539	22,062	10,820	26,337
$5,000-$9,999	1,353	1,502	9,249	16,358	11,312	19,563
$10,000-$14,999	1,298	901	9,529	11,652	11,253	13,566
$15,000-$24,999	1,572	892	16,679	15,162	19,166	17,516
$25,000-$34,999	776	346	12,707	7,547	14,185	8,707
$35,000-$49,999	459	149	10,531	3,895	11,604	4,457
$50,000-$74,999	184	43	5,973	1,382	6,433	1,535
$75,000 and over	72	12	3,274	509	3,446	565
median income	$13,470	$7,532	$21,170	$10,317	$20,293	$10,070
mean income	$17,452	$10,587	$27,142	$14,138	$26,041	$13,913

Mean income by:

work experience
worked at full-time jobs	$19,414	$14,750	$30,498	$19,269	$29,524	$19,010
worked 50-52 weeks	22,859	17,760	34,300	22,198	33,334	21,977

educational attainment
less than 8 years of school	$13,448	$8,269	$15,057	$8,598	$14,914	$8,602
high school graduates	20,400	13,212	25,520	13,955	24,727	13,999
1-3 years of college	25,468	17,852	31,235	17,148	30,340	17,188
4 or more years of college	32,398	20,061	45,709	25,230	44,864	25,388

age
15-24 years old	$9,257	$6,444	$8,915	$7,161	$8,693	$6,998
25-34 years old	17,895	11,262	25,442	15,317	24,365	14,955
35-44 years old	22,419	14,015	35,723	17,724	34,468	17,667
45-54 years old	22,624	13,393	38,632	17,845	37,182	17,831
55-64 years old	21,618	10,117	33,396	14,159	31,899	13,834
65 years old and over	12,280	6,496	20,918	11,864	20,011	11,441

continued on the next page

Table 8.12 continued

	Hispanic		White		Total	
	male	female	male	female	male	female
Mean income by:						
marital status						
single	$12,286	$10,149	$16,902	$14,504	$16,112	$13,656
married	20,462	10,711	32,362	13,828	31,488	13,858
spouse present	21,316	10,896	32,627	13,805	31,888	13,883
spouse absent	13,428	9,700	25,396	14,255	23,158	13,508
widowed	11,504	9,337	18,528	13,822	17,440	13,190
divorced	22,070	14,471	26,830	19,448	25,787	19,058

SOURCE: U.S. Bureau of the Census, Current Population Reports: Money Income of Households, Families, and Persons in the United States: March 1990, Series P-60, #174, pp. 104-105, table 24; p. 108, table 25; pp. 112-119, table 26; pp. 124-127, table 28; pp. 128-149, table 29; pp. 160-163, table 31. C3.186/2:990

NOTES: 'Total' includes other races and ethnic groups not shown separately. Number of persons as of March of the following year. Data is based on persons living in households. Persons with incomes under $5,000 includes those with a loss. Occupation represents the longest job held by the person during the year. Educational attainment covers persons 25 years old and older; income covers persons 15 years old and older.

UNITS: Number of persons and persons with income, in thousands of persons; percent as a percent as shown; mean and median income in current dollars.

Table 8.13 Money Income of Persons 15 Years Old and Older, by Selected Characteristic, 1997

	Hispanic		White		Total	
	male	female	male	female	male	female
Number of persons	10,944	10,485	85,219	89,489	101,123	108,168
persons with incomes:						
under $5,000	1,069	1,959	6,903	15,500	8,578	18,456
$5,000-$9,999	1,490	1,976	7,527	15,597	9,598	19,077
$10,000-$14,999	1,824	1,384	8,979	11,890	10,695	14,123
$15,000-$24,999	2,338	1,415	14,962	16,060	17,800	19,472
$25,000-$34,999	1,237	668	12,678	9,898	14,740	11,813
$35,000-$49,999	890	441	12,602	6,950	14,367	8,207
$50,000-$74,999	487	152	9,829	3,727	10,938	4,351
$75,000 and over	250	61	6,921	1,730	7,451	1,947
median income	$16,216	$10,260	$26,115	$13,792	$25,212	$13,703
mean income	$22,392	$14,509	$36,282	$19,792	$34,794	$19,511

SOURCE: U.S. Bureau of the Census, Current Population Reports, Money Income in the United States: 1997, Series P-60, #200, pp. 30-32, table 8. <www.census.gov/prod/3/98pubs/p60-28900.pdf>, accessed 15 October 1998.

NOTES: 'Total' includes other races and ethnic groups not shown separately. Number of persons as of March of the following year.

UNITS: Number of persons and persons with income, in thousands of persons; mean and median income in current dollars.

Table 8.14 Earnings of Persons, by Sex, by Type of Hispanic Origin, 1997

	type of origin					
	Mexican	Puerto Rican	Cuban	Central/ South Amer	other Hispanic	total Hispanic
1997						
Males	100.0%	100.0%	100.0%	100.0%	100.0%	100.0%
percent with incomes of:						
less than $10,000.	27.4	22.7	21.6	23.0	25.8	25.9
$10,000. to $24,999.	46.5	37.1	31.7	49.5	35.2	44.7
$25,000. to $49,999.	21.1	32.1	32.2	21.1	27.2	23.0
$50,000 or more	5.0	8.0	14.5	6.4	11.8	6.4
Females	100.0%	100.0%	100.0%	100.0%	100.0%	100.0%
percent with incomes of:						
less than $10,000.	44.7	37.6	28.7	36.3	39.4	41.2
$10,000. to $24,999.	40.5	37.6	41.9	45.0	40.2	41.1
$25,000. to $49,999.	12.8	21.5	21.7	15.3	17.2	15.0
$50,000 or more	2.0	3.2	7.8	3.4	3.2	2.7

SOURCE: U.S. Bureau of the Census, "Hispanic Population of the US. (Tables 2.4, 2.6) March, 1997 CPS: Earnings of Persons by Race-Ethnicity Age 15 and over (Detailed Categories)-Values/Percents". Released 7 August 1998.
http://www.census.gov/population/socdemo/hispanic/cps97/tab02-04.txt
http://www.census.gov/population/socdemo/hispanic/cps97/tab02-06.txt

NOTES: 'Other Hispanic origin' includes persons from Spain and persons identifying themselves generally as Hispanic, Spanish, Spanish-American, Hispano, Latino, etc. Persons 15 years old and older.

UNITS: Percent as a percent of total shown (100.0%), mean earnings in current dollars.

Table 8.15 Per Capita Money Income in Current and Constant Dollars, 1980 - 1992

	Hispanic	White	Total
Current dollars			
1980	$ 4,865	$ 8,233	$ 7,787
1985	6,613	11,671	11,013
1986	7,000	12,352	11,670
1987	7,653	13,143	12,391
1988	7,956	13,896	13,123
1989	8,390	14,896	14,056
1990	8,424	15,265	14,387
1991	8,662	15,510	14,617
1992	8,874	15,981	15,033
Constant dollars			
1980	$ 8,294	$14,035	$13,275
1985	8,623	15,218	14,360
1986	8,961	15,812	14,939
1987	9,452	16,232	15,303
1988	9,436	16,480	15,563
1989	9,493	16,854	15,904
1990	9,043	16,386	15,444
1991	8,923	15,977	15,057
1992	8,874	15,981	15,033

SOURCE: U.S. Bureau of the Census, <u>Current Population Reports: Money Income of Households, Families, and Persons in the United States: March 1992</u>, Series P-60, #184, p. B 38, table B-19. C3.186/2:992

NOTES: 'Total' includes other races and ethnic groups not shown separately.

UNITS: Median money income per capita in current and dollars, as shown.

Table 8.16 Families Below the Poverty Level, 1980 - 1997

	Hispanic	White	Total
Number below the poverty level			
1980	751	4,195	6,217
1985	1,074	4,983	7,223
1986	1,085	4,811	7,023
1987	1,168	4,567	7,005
1988	1,141	4,471	6,874
1989	1,133	4,409	6,784
1990	1,244	4,622	7,098
1991	1,372	5,022	7,712
1992	1,529	5,255	8,144
1993	1,625	5,452	8,393
1994	1,724	5,312	8,053
1995	1,695	4,994	7,532
1996	1,748	5,059	7,708
1997	1,721	4,990	7,324
Percent below the poverty level			
1980	23.2%	8.0%	10.3%
1985	25.5	9.1	11.4
1986	24.7	8.6	10.9
1987	25.5	8.1	10.7
1988	23.7	7.9	10.4
1989	23.4	7.8	10.3
1990	25.0	8.1	10.7
1991	26.5	8.8	11.5
1992	26.7	9.1	11.9
1993	27.3	9.4	12.3
1994	27.8	9.1	11.6
1995	27.0	8.5	10.8
1996	26.4	8.6	11.0
1997	24.7	8.4	10.3

SOURCE: U.S. Bureau of the Census, Current Population Reports: Poverty, in the United States:1997, Series P-60, #201, pp. C-8-C-11, table C-3. <www.census.gov/prod/3/98pubs/p60-201.pdf>, accessed 15 October 1998

NOTES: 'Total' includes other races and ethnic groups not shown separately. Families as of March of the following year.

UNITS: Number below the poverty level in thousands of families; percent as a percent of all families, by race, as shown.

Table 8.17 Families Below the Poverty Level by Type of Family and Presence of Related Children, 1997

	Hispanic	White	Total
Total Families	6,961	59,515	70,884
Families below poverty level	1,721	4,990	7,324
Married-couple families	836	2,312	2,821
Male householder, no wife present	118	373	508
Female householder, no husband present	767	2,305	3,995
Total families with children under 18 years	3,305	30,060	37,427
Families below poverty level	792	3,895	5,884
Married-couple families	366	1,516	1,863
Male householder, no wife present	27	310	407
Female householder, no husband present	399	2,069	3,614

SOURCE: U.S. Bureau of the Census, <u>Current Population Reports: Poverty in the United States 1997</u>, Series P-60, #201, pp. C-8 - C-13, table C-3, <www.census.gov/prod/3/98pubs/p60-201.pdf>, accessed 15 October 1998.

NOTES: Total' includes other races and ethnic groups not shown separately.

UNITS: Number in thousands of families

Table 8.18 Selected Characteristics of Families Below the Poverty Level, by Type of Hispanic Origin, 1985 and 1997

	Mex-ican	Puerto Rican	Cuban	Central/ South Amer	other Hispanic	total Hispanic
1985						
families						
number	541	260	41	96	52	991
percent below the poverty level	24.1%	41.9%	12.9%	23.6%	15.2%	25.2%
families with householder 65 years old or over						
number	33	3	14	3	6	58
percent below the poverty level	19.2%	na	na	na	na %	19.4%
families with householder not a high school graduate						
number	367	163	25	54	24	633
percent below the poverty level	29.8%	52:6%	17.0%	36.2%	22.0%	32.5%
families with householder female, with husband absent						
number	183	203	22	42	33	483
percent below the poverty level	43.8%	74.4%	na	47.2%	na	53.4%

continued on the next page

Table **8.18** continued

	type of origin					
	Mex-ican	Puerto Rican	Cuban	Central/ South Amer	other Hispanic	total Hispanic
1997						
families						
number	1,111	258	46	183	151	1,748
percent below the poverty level	27.7%	33.1%	12.5%	19.0%	29.3%	26.4%
families with householder 65 years old or over						
number	49	13	13	7	4	87
percent below the poverty level	17.8%	23.3%	14.1%	13.2%	11.2%	16.7%
families with householder not a high school graduate						
number	768	146	25	102	78	1,118
percent below the poverty level	39.4%	51.6%	25.3%	32.1%	48.9%	39.8%

SOURCE: U.S. Bureau of the Census, The Hispanic Population in the United States: March, 1985, pp. 14-15, table 2 (data from U.S. Bureau of the Census, *Current Population Reports*). C 3.186:P-20/422

U.S. Bureau of the Census, "Hispanic Population of the US (Tables 4.8, 4.4, 4.5) March 1997 CPS: Family Poverty by Race-Ethnicity-Values/Percents". Released 7 August 1998.
http://www.census.gov/population/socdemo/hispanic/cps97/tab04-3.txt
http://www.census.gov/population/socdemo/hispanic/cps97/tab04-4.txt
http://www.census.gov/population/socdemo/hispanic/cps97/tab04-5.txt

NOTES: 'Other Hispanic origin' includes persons from Spain and persons identifying themselves generally as Hispanic, Spanish, Spanish-American, Hispano, Latino, etc.

UNITS: Number in thousands of persons; percent as a percent of total shown (100.0%).

Table 8.19 Persons Below the Poverty Level, 1980 - 1997

	Hispanic	White	Total
Number below the poverty level			
1980	3,491	19,699	29,272
1985	5,236	22,860	33,064
1986	5,117	22,183	32,370
1987	5,422	21,195	32,221
1988	5,357	20,715	31,745
1989	5,430	20,785	31,528
1990	6,006	22,326	33,585
1991	6,339	23,747	35,708
1992	7,592	25,259	38,014
1993	8,126	26,226	39,265
1994	8,416	25,379	38,059
1995	8,574	24,423	36,425
1996	8,697	24,650	36,529
1997	8,308	24,396	35,574
Percent below the poverty level			
1980	25.7%	10.2%	13.0%
1985	29.0	11.4	14.0
1986	27.3	11.0	13.6
1987	28.0	10.4	13.4
1988	26.7	10.1	13.0
1989	26.2	10.0	12.8
1990	28.1	10.7	13.5
1991	28.7	11.3	14.2
1992	29.6	11.9	14.8
1993	30.6	12.2	15.1
1994	30.7	11.7	14.5
1995	30.3	11.2	13.8
1996	29.4	11.2	13.7
1997	27.1	11.0	13.3

SOURCE: U.S. Bureau of the Census, Current Population Reports: Poverty , in the United States: 1997, Series P-60, #201 pp. C-1- C-4, table C-1 <www.census.gov/prod/3/98pubs/p60-201.pdf> , accessed 15 October 1998.

NOTES: 'Total' includes other races and ethnic groups not shown separately. 1987 and 1988 data based on revised processing procedures and is not directly comparable to preceding years.

UNITS: Number below the poverty level in thousands of persons; percent as a percent of all persons, by race, as shown.

Table 8.20   Children Below the Poverty Level, 1980 - 1997

	Hispanic	White	Total
Number below the poverty level			
1980	1,749	7,181	11,543
1985	2,606	8,253	13,010
1986	2,507	8,209	12,876
1987	2,670	7,788	12,843
1988	2,631	7,435	12,455
1989	2,603	7,599	12,590
1990	2,865	8,232	13,431
1991	3,094	8,848	14,341
1992	3,637	8,399	15,294
1993	3,873	9,752	15,727
1994	4,075	9,346	15,289
1995	4,080	8,981	14,665
1996	4,237	9,044	14,623
1997	3,972	8,990	14,113
Percent below the poverty level			
1980	33.2%	13.9%	18.3%
1985	40.3	16.2	20.7
1986	37.7	16.1	20.5
1987	39.3	15.3	20.3
1988	37.6	14.5	19.5
1989	36.2	14.8	19.6
1990	38.4	15.9	20.6
1991	40.4	16.8	21.8
1992	40.0	17.4	22.3
1993	40.9	17.8	22.7
1994	41.5	16.9	21.8
1995	40.0	16.2	20.8
1996	40.3	16.3	20.5
1997	36.8	16.1	19.9

SOURCE: U.S. Bureau of the Census, <u>Current Population Reports: Poverty in the United States: 1997</u>, Series P-60, #201, pp. C-5-C-7, table C-2. <www.census.gov/prod/3/98pubs/p60-201.pdf>, accessed 15 october 1998.

NOTES: 'Total' includes other races and ethnic groups not shown separately.

UNITS: Number below the poverty level in thousands of children; percent as a percent of all children, by race, as shown.

Table 8.21 Persons 65 Years Old and Over Below the Poverty Level, 1970 - 1996

	Hispanic	White	Total
Number below the poverty level			
1970	na	4,011	4,793
1979	154	2,911	3,682
1985	219	2,698	3,456
1990	245	2,707	3,658
1991	237	2,802	3,781
1992	269	2,992	3,983
1993	297	2,939	3,755
1994	323	2,846	3,663
1995	342	2,572	3,318
1996	370	2,667	3,428
Percent below the poverty level			
1970	na %	22.6%	24.6%
1979	26.8	13.3	15.2
1985	23.9	11.0	12.6
1990	22.5	10.1	12.2
1991	20.8	10.3	12.4
1992	22.0	10.9	12.9
1993	21.4	10.7	12.2
1994	22.6	10.2	11.7
1995	23.5	9.0	10.5
1996	24.4	9.4	10.8

SOURCE: U.S. Bureau of the Census, Statistical Abstract of the United States, 1994, p. 476, table 731; 1998, p. 478, table 759, C 3.134:9(year)

NOTES: 'Total' includes other races and ethnic groups not shown separately. Persons as of March of following year.

UNITS: Number below the poverty level in thousands of persons; percent as a percent of all persons, by race, as shown.

Table 8.22 Income of Persons from Specified Sources, 1997

	Hispanic	White	Total
All persons, 15 years and over	17,641	161,752	191,615
Number with income from:			
Earnings	14,306	121,516	144,429
Unemployment compensation	673	4,962	6,042
Workers' compensation	201	1,740	2,043
Social Security	2,021	33,217	37,743
SSI (Supplemental Security Income)	733	3,488	5,111
Public assistance (total)	809	2,288	3,758
Veterans' benefits	88	2,007	2,353
Survivors benefits	71	2,172	2,405
Disability benefits	100	1,212	1,508
Pensions	396	13,209	14,611
Interest	4,750	92,812	102,933
Dividends	793	30,596	32,885
Rents, royalties, estates or trusts	537	11,519	12,592
Education	538	6,245	7,817
Child support	448	4,139	5,034
Alimony	22	383	409
Mean income, total from:	$18,793	$27,989	$27,022
Earnings	20,352	29,700	28,754
Unemployment compensation	3,175	2,613	2,626
Workers' compensation	4,344	5,791	5,838
Social Security	6,774	8,480	8,359
SSI (Supplemental Security Income)	4,235	4,370	4,444
Public assistance (total)	3,830	3,108	3,240
Veterans' benefits	7,394	7,157	7,047
Survivors benefits	na	9,847	10,004
Disability benefits	8,510	10,771	10,213
Pensions	9,149	12,274	12,220
Interest	780	1,959	1,869
Dividends	2,721	2,910	2,883
Rents, royalties, estates or trusts	2,709	4,487	4,316
Education	3,345	3,628	3,732
Child support	3,152	3,826	3,643
Alimony	na	10,401	9,923

SOURCE: U.S. Bureau of the Census, <u>Current Population Reports: Money Income in the United States: 1997</u>, Series P60-200, p. 42, table 11. <www.census.gov/prod/3/98pubs/p60-200.pdf>, accessed 15 October 1998.

NOTES: 'Total' includes other races and ethnic groups not shown separately. Persons 15 years old and older as of March the following year

UNITS: Number of persons in thousands

Table 8.23   Income of Households from Specified Sources, 1992

	Hispanic	White	Total
All households	6,626	82,083	96,391
one or more members received:			
Social Security	16.8%	28.5%	27.7%
AFDC or other non-SSI cash assistance	12.1	3.7	5.2
SSI	6.9	3.2	4.1
food stamps	18.7	6.6	8.8
housing assistance	7.9	3.3	4.6
free or reduced-price school lunches	21.8	5.5	7.4
employer subsidized health insurance	43.5	54.3	52.9
Medicare	16.5	26.6	25.9
Medicaid	28.5	10.1	12.8
Mean household income from:			
Social Security	$7,306	$8,980	$8,708
AFDC or other non-SSI cash assistance	4,513	3,444	3,489
SSI	4,336	3,651	3,666
food stamps	1,713	1,430	1,564
housing assistance	2,297	1,957	2,022
free or reduced-price school lunches	605	547	553
employer subsidized health insurance	3,231	3,163	3,139
Medicare	3,116	3,652	3,511
Medicaid	1,558	1,696	1,595

SOURCE: U.S. Bureau of the Census, Current Population Reports: Measuring the Effect of Benefits and Taxes on Income and Poverty: 1992, Series P-60-186RD, pp. 52-54, table 7. C 3.186/P-60/186RD

NOTES: 'Total' includes other races/ethnic groups not shown separately.

UNITS: Number of households in thousands. Percent as a percent of all households, 100.0%. Mean amount of income from specified source per household receiving that source.

Table 8.24 Child Support Payments Agreed to or Awarded Custodial Parents, 1991

	Hispanic	White	Total
All Custodial Parents	1,160	8,319	11,502
Child support agreed to or awarded	410	5,035	6,190
Supposed to receive child support	356	4,357	5,326
Received payments	233	3,340	4,006
Full Payments	144	2,330	2,742
Partial Payments	89	1,011	1,265
Did not receive payments	123	1,017	1,320
All Custodial Mothers	1,043	6,966	9,918
Child support agreed to or awarded	368	4,459	5,542
Supposed to receive child support	324	3,976	4,883
Received payments	221	3,094	3,728
Full Payments	139	2,162	2,552
Partial Payments	82	932	1,176
Did not receive payments	102	882	1,156
All Custodial Fathers	118	1,352	1,584
Child support agreed to or awarded	42	576	648
Supposed to receive child support	32	381	443
Received payments	12	246	278
Full Payments	5	168	189
Partial Payments	7	78	89
Did not receive payments	20	135	164

SOURCE: U.S. Department of Commerce, Current Population Reports, Consumer Income, Series P60-187, <u>Child Support for Custodial Mothers and Fathers: 1991</u>, pp. 13- 16, table 1. C3.186:P-60/187

NOTES: 'Total' includes other races/ethnic-groups not shown separately.

UNITS: Numbers in thousands. Persons 15 years and older with own children under 21 years of age present from absent parents as of spring 1992.

Chapter 9: Crime & Corrections

Table 9.01 Victimization Rates for Personal Crimes, 1997

	Hispanic victims	White victims	all victims
1997			
crimes of violence	43.1	38.3	39.2
rape/sexual assault	1.5	1.4	1.4
robbery	7.3	3.8	4.3
assault	34.3	33.1	33.5
personal theft	2.4	1.4	1.6

SOURCE: U.S. Department of Justice, Bureau of Justice Statistics, Criminal Victimization in the United States, 1997, p. 3, table 1, p. 4, table 2. (data from the *National Crime Victimization Survey*). J29.9/2:997

NOTES: 'All victims' includes victims of other races and ethnic groups not shown separately. Personal crimes include completed and attempted rape, robbery, assault, and larceny, but exclude homicide. *Based on 10 or fewer sample cases.
The National Crime Victimization Survey has been redesigned. Comparisons of estimates of crime based on previous survey procedures (before 1993) are not recommended.

UNITS: Rates per 1,000 persons, 12 years old and over.

Table 9.02 Victimization Rates for Personal Crimes, by Type of Crime, 1994

	Hispanic	White	Total
All personal crimes	**63.3**	**51.5**	**53.1**
Crimes of violence	59.8	49.4	50.8
completed	19.6	13.6	15.0
attempted/threatened	40.2	35.8	35.8
rape/sexual assault	2.6	1.9	2.0
rape/attempted rape	1.6	1.3	1.5
- rape	0.4*	0.7	0.8
- attempted rape	1.3	0.7	0.7
sexual assault	0.9*	0.6	0.5
robbery	9.8	4.8	6.1
completed/property taken	6.7	2.6	3.7
- with injury	2.5	1.0	1.3
- without injury	4.2	1.6	2.4
attempted to take property	3.1	2.2	2.4
- with injury	0.8*	0.5	0.6
- without injury	2.3	1.6	1.8
assault	47.4	42.7	42.7
aggravated	16.2	10.9	11.6
- with injury	4.7	2.8	3.2
- threatened with weapon	11.5	8.1	8.4
simple	31.2	31.8	31.1
- with minor injury	7.2	7.0	6.9
- without injury	24.1	24.8	24.3
purse snatching/pocket picking	3.5	2.1	2.3

SOURCE: U.S. Department of Justice, Bureau of Justice Statistics, Criminal Victimization in the United States, 1994, p. 7, table 2; p. 10, table 5; p. 12, table 7 (data from the *National Crime Victimization Survey*). J 29.9/2:994

NOTES: 'Total' includes other races and ethnic groups not shown separately. *Based on 10 or fewer sample cases. The National Crime Victimization Survey has been redesigned. Comparisons of estimates of crime based on previous survey procedures (before 1993) are not recommended.

UNITS: Rates per 1,000 persons, 12 years old and over.

Table 9.03 Victimization Rates for Property Crimes, by Type of Crime, 1994

	Hispanic households	White households	All households
All property crimes	425.5	302.0	307.6
Household burglary	71.0	51.7	54.4
completed	58.1	43.4	45.4
- forcible entry	28.4	15.1	17.1
- unlawful entry without force	29.7	28.4	28.2
attempted forcible entry	12.9	8.3	9.0
Theft	314.5	234.6	235.8
completed	299.7	224.2	225.6
- less than $50.	101.8	95.7	93.0
- $50-$249	124.1	76.4	78.1
- $250 or more	56.9	40.6	42.2
- amount not available	16.9	11.5	12.3
attempted	14.9	10.4	10.1
Motor vehicle theft	39.9	15.6	17.5
completed	25.5	10.1	11.6
attempted	14.4	5.5	5.9

SOURCE: U.S. Department of Justice, Bureau of Justice Statistics, Criminal
                   Victimization in the United States, 1994, p. 21, tables 16, 17 (data
                   from the *National Crime Victimization Survey*). J 29.9/2:994

NOTES: 'Total' includes other races and ethnic groups not shown separately.
                   The National Crime Victimization Survey has been redesigned. Comparisons
                   of estimates of crime based on previous survey procedures (before 1993) are
                   not recommended.

UNITS: Rates per 1,000 households.

Table 9.04   Criminal History Profile of Prisoners Under Sentence of Death, 1997

	Hispanic	White	Total
U.S. Total	283	1,613	3,335
Prior felony convictions			
Yes	153	939	2,011
No	104	552	1,068
Not reported	0	0	256
Prior homicide convictions			
Yes	22	127	281
No	251	1,457	2,980
Not reported	0	0	74
Legal status at time of capital offense			
Charges pending	16	121	225
Probation	25	141	301
Parole	63	237	578
Prison escapee	2	25	38
Prison inmate	4	35	76
Other status	1	16	30
None	134	872	1,721
Not reported	0	0	366

SOURCE: U.S. Department of Justice, Bureau of Justice Statistics, Capital Punishment, 1997, p. 10, table 9. J 29.11:997

NOTES: 'Total' includes other races and ethnic groups not shown separately. 'White' excludes Hispanic persons.

UNITS: Number of jail inmates. Percent of all jail inmates of given race/ethnic group.

Table 9.05 Prisoners Under Jurisdiction of Federal and State Correctional Authorities, 1994, 1995

	Hispanic	White	Total
December 31, 1994			
Total	156,908	464,167	1,054,774
federal institutions	25,226	58,403	95,034
state institutions	131,682	405,764	959,740
December 31, 1995			
Total	174,292	455,021	1,126,287
federal institutions	27,559	60,261	100,250
state institutions	146,733	394,760	1,026,037

SOURCE: U.S. Department of Justice, Bureau of Justice Statistics, <u>Sourcebook of Criminal Justice Statistics, 1995</u>, pp. 562-563, table 6.26; <u>1996,</u> pp. 524-525, table 6.26 and table 6.27 . J 29.9/6:(YEAR)

NOTES: 'Total' includes other races and ethnic groups not shown separately. 'White' excludes Hispanic persons.

UNITS: Number of prisoners under jurisdictional authority.

Table 9.06 Jail Inmates, 1990-1997

	Hispanic	White	Total
1990	14.3%	41.8%	100%
1991	14.2	41.1	100
1992	14.5	40.1	100
1993	15.1	39.3	100
1994	15.4	39.1	100
1995	14.7	40.1	100
1996	15.6	41.6	100
1997	15.7	40.6	100

SOURCE: U.S. Department of Justice, Bureau of Justice Statistics,
            Prison and Jail Inmates 1997, p. 6, table 7 J 29.11/5:997

NOTES: 'Total' includes other races and ethnic groups not shown
            separately. 'White' excludes Hispanic persons.

UNITS: Percent of local jail inmates.

Table 9.07 Prisoners Under Sentence of Death, by State, 1998

	Hispanic	White	Total
United States	265	1,611	3,387
Alabama	2	91	163
Arizona	18	86	121
Arkansas	1	19	39
California	82	203	494
Colorado	1	1	4
Connecticut	0	2	5
Delaware	0	7	17
Florida	35	203	368
Georgia	1	64	119
Idaho	0	19	19
Illinois	6	53	156
Indiana	1	27	45
Kansas	0	1	1
Kentucky	0	23	30
Louisiana	0	17	72
Maryland	0	3	17
Mississippi	0	28	60
Missouri	0	47	87
Montana	0	6	6
Nebraska	0	9	11
Nevada	8	45	92
New Hampshire	X	X	0
New Jersey	0	8	15
New Mexico	1	3	4
New York	X	X	0
North Carolina	2	85	199
Ohio	3	87	180
Oklahoma	3	69	127
Oregon	2	19	23
Pennsylvania	12	69	216
South Carolina	0	34	73
South Dakota	0	2	2
Tennessee	1	63	96
Texas	80	169	425
Utah	2	7	11
Virginia	1	23	46
Washington	0	15	19
Wyoming	X	X	0

SOURCE: U.S. Department of Justice, Bureau of Justice Statistics, <u>Sourcebook of Criminal Justice Statistics, 1997</u>, p. 527, table 6.76. Data from NAACP Legal Defense and Educational Fund. J 29.9/6:997

NOTES: 'Total' includes other races and ethnic groups not shown separately.

UNITS: Number prisoners under sentence of death.

Table 9.08   Chances of Going to State or Federal Prison

	Hispanic	White	All Races
For the first time, by age			
20	1.5%	0.4%	1.1%
25	3.6	0.9	2.4
30	5.2	1.4	3.3
35	6.3	1.7	4.0
40	7.5	2.0	4.4
45	8.2	2.1	4.7
50	8.8	2.3	4.9
55	9.1	2.4	5.0
65	9.4	2.5	5.1
Lifetime	9.4	2.5	5.1
At some time during the rest of life, by age			
birth	9.4%	2.5%	5.1%
20	8.7	2.3	4.5
25	6.4	1.7	3.1
30	4.9	1.2	2.1
35	3.8	0.9	1.4
40	2.3	0.6	0.9
45	1.6	0.4	0.6

SOURCE: U.S. Department of Justice, Bureau of Justice Statistics, <u>Lifetime Likelihood of Going to State or Federal Prision</u>,March 1997, pp. 2-3, tables 1, 2 . J 29.11/8:997

NOTES: Chances of going to State or Federal Prison for the first time are cumulative percents. These estimates were obtained by sequentially applying age-specific first-incarceration rates and mortality rates for each group to a hypothetical population of 100,000 births. Changes of going to State or Federal Prison at some time are for persons not previously incarcerated. These estimates were obtained by subtracting the cumulative percent first incarcerated for each age from the lifetime likelihood of incarceration. 'White' and 'Black' exclude persons of Hispanic origin.

UNITS: Percent of all resident population.

Table 9.09 Attitudes Toward Crime and Safety, 1996

Question: I want to ask you how much you worry about each of the following situations.
Do you worry very frequently, somewhat frequently, seldom, or never about...?

	Hispanic	White	Total
Getting murdered:			
very frequently	32.5%	6.3%	10.6%
somewhat frequently	2.6	12.2	12.4
seldom	26.0	41.4	38.4
never	39.0	40.1	38.6
Getting beaten up, knifed or shot:			
very frenquently	29.5%	9.0%	12.5%
somewhat frequently	17.9	20.1	20.3
seldom	29.5	43.2	40.2
never	23.1	27.7	27.1
Yourself or someone in your family getting sexually assaulted:			
very frequently	40.0%	14.2%	18.1%
somewhat frequently	17.3	31.1	29.0
seldom	18.7	34.7	32.1
never	24.0	20.0	20.8
Your home being burglarized:			
very frenquently	47.4%	17.6%	20.4%
somewhat frequently	19.2	28.9	28.9
seldom	14.1	36.7	34.1
never	19.2	16.9	16.7

SOURCE: U.S. Department of Justice, Bureau of Justice Statistics, <u>Sourcebook of Criminal Justice Statistics, 1997</u>, p. 126, table 2.40. (Data provided by Survey Research Program, College of Criminal Justice, Sam Houston State University) J 29.9/6:997

NOTES: The National Opinion Survey on Crime and Justice - 1996 was designed and commissions by the College of Criminal Justice's Survey Research Program at Sam Houston State University. The data were collected by the Public Policy Research Institute of Texas A&M University through telephone interviews conducted from May 16 to June 9, 1996. A total of 1,085 interviews were conducted from a stratified random sample of all working telephone numbers in the United States. The data presented are weighted estimates adjusted according to U.S. Bureau of the Census racial/ethnic group and gender population figures for 1990.

UNITS: Percent of persons taking survey who answered with given response.

Table 9.10 Attitudes Toward the Death Penalty, 1996

Question: Are you in favor of the death penalty for persons convicted of murder?

	Hispanic	White	All Races
Yes	61.0%	77.2%	73.4%
No	33.8	16.5	19.9
Don't know/refused	5.2	6.3	6.7

Question: If you knew that murderers would be given a true life sentence without the possibility of parole, would you continue to favor the death penalty?

	Hispanic	White	All Races
Yes	74.5%	77.5%	75.7%
No	21.3	18.2	20.1
Don't know	4.3	3.8	3.9

SOURCE: U.S. Department of Justice, Bureau of Justice Statistics, <u>Sourcebook of Criminal Justice Statistics, 1997,</u> (Data provided by the Survey Research Program, College of Criminal Justice, Sam Houston State University, p. 139, tables 2.58 and 2.59. 29.9/6:997

NOTES: The National Opinion Survey on Crime and Justice - 1996 was designed and commissions by the College of Criminal Justice's Survey Research Program at Sam Houston State University. The data were collected by the Public Policy Research Institute of Texas A&M University through telephone interviews conducted from May 16 to June 9, 1996. A total of 1,085 interviews were conducted from a stratified random sample of all working telephone numbers in the United States. The data presented are weighted estimates adjusted according to U.S. Bureau of the Census racial/ethnic group and gender population figures for 1990.

UNITS: Percent of persons taking survey who answered with given response.

Table 9.11 HIV-Positive Local Jail Inmates, 1995-96

	Hispanic	White	Total
Tested inmates who reported results	45,759	110,023	289,991
male	40,985	98,745	258,019
female	4,774	11,278	31,972
HIV-positive	3.2%	1.4%	2.2%
male	3.5	1.3	2.1
female	1.3	2.1	2.4

SOURCE: U.S. Department of Justice, Bureau of Justice Statistics, <u>HIV in Prisons and Jails, 1995</u>, p. 8, table 7.

NOTES: 'Total' includes other races/ethnic groups not shown separately.

UNITS: Percent of inmates tested for HIV (Human Immunodeficiency Virus) and reporting the results.

Table 9.12 Victimization Rates for Personal Crimes, by Sex of the Victim, 1994

	Hispanic		White		Total	
	male	female	male	female	male	female
All personal crimes	**na**	**na**	**60.4**	**43.1**	**61.7**	**45.1**
Crimes of violence	68.1	51.8	58.6	40.7	59.7	42.5
completed	22.3	17.1	14.2	13.0	16.0	14.1
attempted/threatened	45.8	34.7	44.4	27.6	43.7	28.4
rape/sexual assault	0.0*	5.0	0.2	3.5	0.2	3.7
robbery	12.6	7.2	6.5	3.2	8.1	4.1
completed/property taken	9.1	4.5	3.3	2.0	4.7	2.8
- with injury	3.2	1.9*	1.2	0.9	1.7	1.0
- without injury	5.9	2.6	2.1	1.1	3.0	1.8
attempted to take property	3.5	2.7	3.3	1.2	3.4	1.3
- with injury	0.6*	0.9*	0.8	0.4	0.7	0.4
- without injury	2.9	1.8*	2.5	0.8	2.7	0.9
assault	55.5	39.6	51.8	34.0	51.3	34.7
aggravated	21.8	10.8	14.6	7.4	15.3	8.1
- with injury	5.9	3.5	3.3	2.3	3.9	2.5
- threatened with weapon	15.9	7.3	11.2	5.1	11.4	5.6
simple	33.7	28.9	37.2	26.6	36.0	26.6
- with minor injury	7.2	7.1	7.5	6.5	7.2	6.5
- without injury	26.5	21.8	29.7	20.1	28.7	20.1
purse snatching/pocket picking	1.5*	5.4	1.8	2.4	2.0	2.5

SOURCE: U.S. Department of Justice, Bureau of Justice Statistics, Criminal Victimization in the United States, 1994, p. 7, table 2; p. 11, table 6, p. 13, table 8 (data from the *National Crime Victimization Survey*). J 29.9/2:994

NOTES: 'Total' includes other races/ethnic groups not shown separately. *Based on 10 or fewer sample cases.
The National Crime Victimization Survey has been redesigned. Comparisons of estimates of crime based on previous surveyprocedures (before 1993) are not recommended

UNITS: Rates per 1,000 persons, 12 years old and over.

Chapter 10: Special Topics

Table 10.01   AIDS (Acquired Immunodeficiency Syndrome) Cases,
                     by Sex and Age, 1985 - 1997

	Hispanic	White	Total
All years*			
children under 13 years old	1,465	1,399	7,526
persons over 13 years old			
male	73,718	256,246	496,642
female	14,470	21,311	87,976
1985			
children under 13 years old	18	26	128
persons over 13 years old			
male	990	4,756	7,509
female	100	141	524
1990			
children under 13 years old	168	159	723
persons over 13 years old			
male	4,769	20,894	36,314
female	733	1,225	4,532
1992			
children under 13 years old	129	128	749
persons over 13 years old			
male	5,624	20,832	39,069
female	1,014	1,468	5,953
1993			
children under 13 years old	175	151	871
persons over 13 years old			
male	12,641	43,346	85,393
female	2,627	4,048	15,947

continued on the next page

Table 10.01 continued

	Hispanic	White	Total
1994			
children under 13 years old	181	143	972
persons over 13 years old			
male	10,111	29,556	62,935
female	2,283	3,090	13,330
1995			
children under 13 years old	136	117	747
persons over 13 years old			
male	9,198	26,260	57,231
female	2,237	3,067	13,061
1996			
children under 13 years old	127	96	656
persons over 13 years old			
male	8,622	23,270	52,781
female	2,077	2,875	13,222
1997 (January-June)			
children under 13 years old	51	35	266
persons over 13 years old			
male	4,138	9,164	23,336
female	1,061	1,327	6,551

SOURCE: U.S. Department of Health and Human Services, <u>Health United States, 1998</u>, p. 265, table 55 (data from Centers for Disease Control, Center for Infectious Diseases, Division of HIV/AIDS. HE 20.6223:998

NOTES: 'Total Races' includes other races/ethnic groups not shown separately. 'White' excludes white Hispanics. Data excludes residents of U.S. Territories. Historic data is revised continually on an ongoing basis. Data for all years have been updated through September 30, 1993. *'All years' includes cases prior to 1985.

UNITS: Number of cases known to the Centers for Disease Control, by year of report; percent distribution as a percent of total (100.0%).

Table 10.02   Death rates for Human Immunodeficiency Virus (HIV)
infection, 1987 - 1996

	Hispanic		White		Total	
	male	female	male	female	male	female
1987	17.8	2.1	8.4	0.6	10.0	1.1
1988	20.3	3.1	10.0	0.7	12.1	1.4
1989	27.0	4.0	13.2	0.9	15.8	1.8
1990	27.2	3.7	15.0	1.1	17.7	2.1
1991	30.1	4.8	16.7	1.3	20.1	2.7
1992	33.0	5.6	18.1	1.6	22.3	3.2
1993	33.6	6.5	19.0	1.9	24.1	3.8
1994	39.3	7.7	20.1	2.3	26.4	4.8
1995	39.0	8.5	19.6	2.5	26.2	5.2
1996	26.0	6.2	12.5	1.8	18.1	4.2

SOURCE: U.S. Department of Health and Human Services, Health United States, 1998, p. 243, table 44 (data from Centers for Disease Control and Prevention, National Center for Health Statistics. HE 20.6223:998

NOTES: 'Total' includes other races/ethnic groups not shown separately.
'White' excludes white Hispanics. Data excludes residents of U.S. Territories

UNITS: Number of deaths known to the Centers for Disease Control, by year of report.

Table 10.03 AIDS (Acquired Immunodeficiency Syndrome) Cases, by Transmission Category, 1985 - 1996

	Hispanic	White	Total
All years*, all transmission categories	88,188	277,557	584,618
men who have sex with men	35,535	193,985	295,355
injecting drug use	30,673	32,092	144,567
men who have sex with men and			
injecting drug use	4,523	20,377	37,514
hemophilia/coagulation disorder	351	3,531	4,508
heterosexual contact	8,722	12,206	50,356
heterosexual contact with			
injecting drug user	3,905	5,068	21,114
transfusion	817	4,774	7,860
undetermined	7,567	10,592	44,458
1985, all transmission categories	1,090	4,897	8,033
men who have sex with men	547	3,983	5,357
injecting drug use	394	246	1,387
men who have sex with men and			
injecting drug use	83	409	655
hemophilia/coagulation disorder	7	59	71
heterosexual contact	27	33	151
heterosexual contact with			
injecting drug user	24	18	107
transfusion	6	125	166
undetermined	26	42	246

continued on the next page

Table 10.03   continued

	Hispanic	White	Total
1990, all transmission categories	5,502	22,119	40,846
men who have sex with men	2,469	16,589	23,826
injecting drug use	2,014	2,059	9,280
men who have sex with men and			
injecting drug use	320	1,562	2,804
hemophilia/coagulation disorder	28	280	348
heterosexual contact	376	650	2,261
heterosexual contact with			
injecting drug user	281	352	1,495
transfusion	83	512	788
undetermined	212	467	1,539
1996, all transmission categories	10,699	26,145	66,003
men who have sex with men	3,682	16,349	27,316
injecting drug use	3,296	3,692	16,405
men who have sex with men and			
injecting drug use	348	1,517	3,044
hemophilia/coagulation disorder	33	211	321
heterosexual contact	1,430	1,856	8,609
heterosexual contact with			
injecting drug user	467	633	2,647
transfusion	86	221	548
undetermined	1,824	2,245	9,760

SOURCE: U.S. Department of Health and Human Services, <u>Health United States, 1998</u>,
p. 266, table 56 (data from Centers for Disease Control, Center for
Infectious Diseases, Division of HIV/AIDS.Prevention) HE 20.6223:998

NOTES: 'Total' includes other races/ethnic groups not shown separately. 'White'
excludes White Hispanics. Data excludes cases of residents of U.S.
Territories. 'Hemophilia' includes coagulation disorders. 'Heterosexual'
includes persons who have had heterosexual contact with a person with
AIDS, or at risk of AIDS, and persons without other identified risks who
were born in countries where heterosexual transmission is believed to play
a major role although precise means of transmission have not yet been fully
determined. Data are updated through June 30, 1995. *'All years'
includes cases prior to 1985.

UNITS: Number of cases known to the Centers for Disease Control, by year of report.

Table 10.04   Vaccinations of Children 19-35 Months of Age for Selected
Diseases, 1996

	Hispanic	White	Total
1996			
combined series (4:3:1:3)	71%	79%	77%
DTP (4 doses or more)	77	83	81
Polio (3 doses or more)	89	92	91
Measles-containing	88	92	91
Hib (3 doses or more)	89	93	92
Hepatitus B (3 doses or more)	80	82	82

SOURCE: U.S. Department of Health and Human Services, Health United States, 1998, p.
261, table 52 (Centers for Disease Control and Prevention, National Center for
Health Statistics and National Immunization Program. Data from the National
Immunization Survey) HE 20.6223:993

NOTES: 'Total' includes other races/ethnic groups not shown separately. 'White' excludes
White Hispanics. Data excludes cases of residents of U.S. Territories.
The 4:3:1:3 combined series consists of 4 doses of diphtheria-tetanus-pertussis
(DTP) vaccine, 3 doses of polio vaccine, 1 dose of a measles-containing
vaccine, and 3 doses of Haemophilus influenzae type b (Hib) vaccine.
DPT is the Diphtheria-tetanus-pertussis vaccine.
Hib is the Haemophilus influenzae type b (Hib) vaccine.

UNITS: Percent of children 19-35 months of age.

Table 10.05   Health Insurance Coverage, 1990, 1997

	Hispanic	White	Total
Not covered by private or government health insurance			
total, 1990	28.2%	12.0%	12.9%
total, 1997	34.2%	15.0%	16.1%
children under 18 years	28.6%	14.1%	15.0%

SOURCE: U.S. Bureau of the Census, <u>Current Population Reports: Household Economic Studies - Health Insurance Coverage: 1987-1990</u>, Series P-70, #29, p. 19, table 1 C 3.186/P-70/29 ; <u>Current Population Reports: Consumer Income - Health Insurance Coverage 1997</u>, Series P-60-202, p. 2, figure 2, p. 3, figure 5. <www.census.gov/prod/3/98pubs/p60-202.pdf>, accessed 15 October 1998.

NOTES: 'Total' includes other races and ethnic groups not shown separately.

UNITS: Percent as a percent of all persons in households, 100.0%.

Table 10.06   Selected Characteristics of Farms and Farm Operators, 1992

	Hispanic farms	All farms
Characteristics of farms		
Farms and land in farms		
farms (number)	20,956	1,925,300
land in farms (acres)	12,394,690	945,531,506
harvested cropland (acres)	1,836,951	295,936,976
Farms by size		
1-9 acres	3,618	166,496
10-49 acres	5,733	387,711
50-139 acres	3,783	445,055
140-219 acres	1,822	233,628
220-499 acres	2,419	333,111
500 acres or more	3,581	359,299
Owned and rented land in farms		
owned land in farms		
farms	18,187	1,708,395
acres	6,668,784	540,695,158
rented or leased land in farms		
farms	8,023	813,564
acres	5,725,906	404,836,348
Market value of agricultural products sold, (in thousands of dollars)		
total	$2,414,128	$162,608,334
crops (including nursery and greenhouse crops)	1,388,363	75,228,255
livestock, poultry and their products	1,025,765	87,380,078
Farms by value of sales		
less than $1,000	3,854	212,580
$2,500-$9,999	3,098	210,187
$2,500-$9,999	5,567	483,750
$10,000-$19,999	2,164	232,067
$20,000-$24,000	609	69,737
$25,000 or more	5,664	716,979

continued on the next page

Table 10.06 continued

	Hispanic farms	All farms
Farms by Standard Industrial Classification		
cash grains (011)	1,414	405,008
field crops except cash grains (013)	2,337	250,338
cotton (0131)	473	20,447
tobacco (0132)	225	90,826
sugarcane and sugarbeets; Irish potatoes; field crops except cash grains not elsewhere classified (0133, 0134, 0139)	1,639	139,065
vegetables and melons (016)	980	29,605
fruits and tree nuts (017)	3,207	89,514
horticultural specialties (018)	728	39,712
general farms, primarily crop (019)	481	48,847
livestock, except dairy, poultry and animal specialties (021)	9,688	808,283
beef cattle, except feedlots (0212)	8,158	612,203
dairy farms (024)	530	113,412
poultry and eggs (025)	323	35,066
animal specialties (027)	996	80,504
general farms, primarily livestock and animal specialties (029)	272	25,011

Characteristics of the farm operator

	Hispanic farms	All farms
Residence		
on farm operated	12,875	1,378,701
not on farm operated	7,765	408,560
not reported	316	138,039
Principal occupation		
farming	10,414	1,053,150
other	10,542	872,150
Days of work off farm		
none	7,883	801,881
any	12,195	992,773

continued on the next page

Table 10.06   continued

Characteristics of the farm operator - continued	Hispanic farms	All farms
Days of work off farm - continued		
1-99 days	2,567	165,180
100-199 days	2,285	162,023
200 days or more	7,343	665,570
Years on present farm		
2 years or less	1,760	94,711
3 or 4 years	2,316	133,079
5 to 9 years	3,737	258,767
10 years or more	10,514	1,112,827
average on present farm	15.3	19.5
Age		
under 25 years old	230	27,906
25-34 years old	1,820	178,826
35-44 years old	4,428	381,746
45-54 years old	5,108	429,333
55-59 years old	2,440	213,315
60-64 years old	2,428	216,524
65-69 years old	1,899	188,165
70 years old and over	2,603	289,475
average age	52.7	53.3
Sex		
male	19,165	1,780,144
female	1,791	145,156

SOURCE: U.S. Bureau of the Census, <u>1992 Census of Agriculture</u>, Vol. 1
Geographic Area Series, Pt. 51, U.S. Summary and State Data, pp.
23-24, table 17. C 3.31/4:992/v. 1/ pt. 51

NOTES: 'All farms' includes farms owned/operated by persons of all races.

UNITS: Farms, farms by size, farms by organization, farms by value of sales,
farms by Standard Industrial Classification, in number of farms; land
in farms and harvested crop lands in acres; market value of
agricultural products sold in thousands of dollars. Characteristics of
farm operators in number of farm operators.

Table 10.07   Summary of Results of the 1996 Consumer Expenditure
Survey

	Hispanic consumer units	White consumer units	All consumer units
Number of consumer units	8,717	91,856	104,212
income before taxes	$29,166	$39,419	$38,014
income after taxes	$27,449	$36,052	$34,864
Average number in consumer unit:			
persons	3.4	2.5	2.5
children under 18 years old	1.3	0.6	0.7
persons 65 and over	0.2	0.3	0.3
earners	1.5	1.4	1.3
vehicles	1.6	2.0	1.9
Average annual expenditures			
Total	$27,868	$34,994	$33,797
food	4,862	4,844	4,698
food at home	3,375	2,918	2,876
- cereals and bakery products	483	457	447
cereals and cereal products	209	167	166
bakery products	274	290	281
- meats, poultry, fish, and eggs	976	718	737
beef	317	213	215
pork	200	149	157
other meats	109	99	99
poultry	192	139	144
fish and seafood	93	85	88
eggs	64	34	34
- dairy products	363	326	312
fresh milk and cream	178	138	132
other dairy products	185	188	180
- fruits and vegetables	639	499	490
fresh fruits	217	158	153
fresh vegetables	209	151	147
processed fruits	129	110	110
processed vegetables	83	81	80

continued on the next page

Table 10.07   continued

	Hispanic consumer units	White concumer units	All consumer units
food at home - continued			
- other food at home	$ 913	$ 918	$ 889
sugar and other sweets	104	117	114
fats and oils	100	83	83
miscellaneous foods	393	404	391
nonalcoholic beverages	282	260	252
- food prepared by consumer unit on			
out of town trips	34	54	49
food away from home	1,488	1,926	1,823
alcoholic beverages	237	329	309
housing	$ 9,208	$11,046	$10,747
shelter	5,512	6,237	6,064
- owned dwellings	2,456	4,015	3,783
mortgage interest and charges	1,601	2,237	2,114
property taxes	498	1,005	939
maintenance, repair, insurance, other	357	773	729
- rented dwellings	2,871	1,767	1,864
- other lodging	185	455	417
utilities, fuels and public services	2,139	2,335	2,347
- natural gas	228	284	291
- electricity	725	905	907
- fuel oil and other fuels	65	115	108
- telephone	870	757	772
- water and other public services	251	273	268
household operations	316	545	522
- personal services	195	260	259
- other household expenses	121	284	263
housekeeping supplies	375	486	464
- laundry and cleaning supplies	145	120	119
- other household products	154	217	205
- postage and stationary	76	149	140

continued on the next page

Table 10.07   continued

	Hispanic consumer units	White consumer units	All consumer units
household furnishings and equipment	$ 866	$ 1,443	$ 1,350
- household textiles	59	80	76
- furniture	291	337	321
- floor coverings	25	111	101
- major appliances	146	170	162
- small appliances, misc. housewares	69	90	84
- misc. household equipment	276	656	607
apparel and services	$ 1,915	$ 1,711	$ 1,752
- men and boys	437	420	423
men, 16 years old and over	320	334	330
boys, 2-15 years old	117	86	93
- women and girls	728	716	718
women, 16 years old and over	570	613	607
girls, 2-15 years old	157	102	111
- children under 2 years old	125	79	82
- footwear	422	271	298
- other apparel and services	204	226	230
transportation	$ 5,340	$ 6,659	$ 6,382
- vehicle purchases	2,316	2,956	2,815
cars and trucks (new) net outlay	936	1,281	1,209
cars and trucks (used) net outlay	1,378	1,632	1,568
other vehicles	2	43	38
- gasoline and motor oil	1,040	1,125	1,082
- other vehicle expenses	1,663	2,129	2,058
vehicle finance charges	215	277	276
maintenance and repairs	603	669	645
vehicle insurance	557	719	698
vehicle rental, license and other charges	288	464	440
- public transportation	321	449	427

continued on the next page

Table 10.07   continued

	Hispanic consumer units	White consumer units	All consumer units
health care	$ 1,035	$ 1,872	$ 1,770
- health insurance	488	863	827
- medical services	317	587	543
- drugs	175	319	303
- medical supplies	55	103	97
entertainment	$ 1,087	$ 1,963	1,834
- fees and admissions	209	498	459
- televisions, radios, sound equipment	463	572	561
- pets, toys, playground equipment	200	360	335
- other entertainment equipment, supplies and services	216	533	479
personal care products and services	$ 489	$ 500	$ 513
reading	70	171	159
education	283	551	524
tobacco products and smoking supplies	139	264	255
miscellaneous	656	891	855
cash contributions	363	986	940
personal insurance and pensions	2,185	3,208	3,060
- life and other personal insurance	226	355	353
- pensions and Social Security	1,960	2,854	2,707

Sources on income and personal taxes

	Hispanic consumer units	White consumer units	All consumer units
Money income before taxes	$ 29,166	$ 39,419	$ 38,014
wages and salaries	24,314	30,546	29,560
self employment income	1,176	2,540	2,318
Social Security, private and government retirement	1,965	4,551	4,334

continued on the next page

Table 10.07   continued

	Hispanic consumer units	White consumer units	All consumer units
Money income before taxes - continued			
interest, dividends, rental income, other property income	$ 135	$ 844	$ 761
unemployment, workers' compensation, veterans benefits	264	222	213
public assistance, supplemental security income, food stamps	969	321	437
regular contributions for support	151	245	243
other income	193	150	148
Personal taxes	$ 1,718	$ 3,367	$ 3,150
federal income taxes	1,338	2,542	2,372
state income taxes	361	703	665
other taxes	19	121	113
Income after taxes	$ 27,449	$ 36,052	$ 34,864

SOURCE: U.S. Department of Labor, Bureau of Labor Statistics, <u>Consumer Expenditure Survey, 1996</u>, table 7, accessed 15 October 1998, < ftp://ftp.bls.gov/pub/special.requests/ce/standard/1996/tenracar.txt >

NOTES: 'All consumer units' includes consumer units of all races and ethnic groups.

UNITS: Number of consumer units in thousands; average numbers as shown; average annual expenditures by category, average income by source of income, and addenda, averages in current dollars.

Table 10.08   Occupied Housing Units, by Tenure, 1980 and 1995

	Black householder	White householder	Householders of all races
1980			
All households	4,008	68,810	80,390
owner occupied			
number	1,739	46,671	51,795
percent	43.4%	67.8%	64.4%
renter occupied	2,269	22,139	28,595
1995			
All households	7,757	81,611	97,693
owner occupied			
number	3,245	56,507	63,544
percent	41.8%	69.2%	65.0%
renter occupied	4,512	25,104	34,150

SOURCE: U.S. Bureau of the Census, Statistical Abstract of the United States, 1998, p. 725, table 1214.   C 3.134:998

NOTES: 'Total' includes persons of all races/ethnic groups. Persons of Hispanic origin can be of any race.

UNITS: Number of housing units; percent as a percent of total as shown.

Table 10.09   Housing Affordability: Families and Unrelated Individuals, 1991

	Hispanic	White	Total
Percent that cannot afford a median priced home in their region using conventional, fixed rate, 30 year financing			
All families	78.8%	47.0%	51.3%
married couples	71.0	40.2	42.2
male householder (no wife present)	86.6	64.7	67.8
female householder (no husband present)	94.3	79.4	83.9
Unrelated individuals	93.1	73.9	76.2
Percent that cannot afford a median priced home in their region using FHA, fixed rate, 30 year financing			
All families	77.6%	45.0%	49.4%
married couples	69.4	37.9	39.9
male householder (no wife present)	86.6	63.7	66.7
female householder (no husband present)	93.8	78.6	83.3
Unrelated individuals	92.3	73.1	75.5

continued on the next page

Table 10.09   continued

	Hispanic	White	Total
Percent that cannot afford a modestly priced home in their region using conventional, fixed rate, 30 year financing			
All families	71.1%	37.9%	42.4%
married couples	61.4	31.1	33.0
male householder (no wife present)	80.7	54.8	57.5
female householder (no husband present)	90.5	70.2	76.1
Unrelated individuals	87.8	63.6	66.6
Percent that cannot afford a modestly priced home in their region using FHA, fixed rate, 30 year financing			
All families	68.7%	34.6%	39.3%
married couples	57.9	27.4	29.4
male householder (no wife present)	80.7	53.4	55.9
female householder (no husband present)	90.0	68.7	74.8
Unrelated individuals	86.8	61.7	64.8

SOURCE: U.S. Bureau of the Census, <u>Current Housing Reports: Who Can Afford to Buy A House in 1991?</u>, p. 2-9, table 2-2; p. 3-8, table 3-2.   C 3.215:H121/93-3

NOTES: 'Total' includes families/unrelated individuals of all races/ethnic groups.

UNITS: Percent as a percent of families/unrelated individuals as shown.

Table 10.10   Selected Characteristics of Live Births, 1990 - 1996

	Hispanic births	White births	Total births
1990			
birth weight under 2,500 grams	6.06%	5.70%	6.97%
birth weight under 1,500 grams	1.03	0.95	1.27
mother under 18 years old	6.6	3.6	4.7
mother 18-19 years old	10.2	7.3	8.1
births to unmarried mothers	36.7	20.4	28.0
mother with less than 12 years of school	53.9	22.4	23.8
mother with 16 years or more of school	5.1	19.3	17.5
prenatal care began in 1st trimester	60.2	79.2	75.8
prenatal care began in 3rd trimester or no prenatal care	12.0	4.9	6.1
1996			
birth weight under 2,500 grams	6.28%	6.34%	7.39%
birth weight under 1,500 grams	1.12	1.09	1.37
mother under 18 years old	7.3	4.2	5.1
mother 18-19 years old	10.1	7.2	7.9
births to unmarried mothers	40.7	25.7	32.4
mother with less than 12 years of school	51.4	21.6	22.4
mother with 16 years or more of school	6.4	23.9	22.1
prenatal care began in 1st trimester	72.2	84.0	81.9
prenatal care began in 3rd trimester or no prenatal care	6.7	3.3	4.0

SOURCE: U.S. Department of Health and Human Services, <u>Health United States, 1998</u>, p. 176, table 6, p. 177, table 7, p. 178, table 8, p. 179, table 9, p. 181, table 11. HE 20.6223:998

NOTES: Data based on race of the mother. Data on Hispanic-origin available in 48 states plus Washington, DC.

UNITS: Percent, as a percent of all live births, 100.0%.

Table 10.11   Current Users of Cigarettes, Alcohol, Marijuana, and
Cocaine, by Age, 1996

	Hispanic	White	Total
1996			
Cigarettes			
persons 12-17 years old	15%	21%	18%
Alcohol			
persons 12-17 years old	20	20	19
persons 18-25 years old	50	65	60
Marijuana			
persons 12-17 years old	7	7	7
persons 18-25 years old	8	14	13
Cocaine			
persons 12-17 years old	1.1	0.5	0.6
persons 18-25 years old	2.1	2.3	2.0

SOURCE: U.S. Department of Health and Human Services, Health United States,
1998, pp. 275-276, table 64   HE 20.6223:998

NOTES: 'Total' includes other races/ethnic groups not shown separately.
'White''excludes Hispanic persons.

UNITS: Percent as a percent of population by age.

Table 10.12   General Mobility, 1996 to 1997

	Hispanic	White	Total
Total	28,985	217,026	262,976
same house (non-movers)	22,686	182,800	219,585
different house in U.S.	5,859	33,299	42,088
same county	4,659	21,485	27,740
different county	1,199	11,814	14,348
same state	684	6,523	7,960
different state	516	5,291	6,389
same region	232	2,504	3,220
different region	284	2,787	3,168
movers from abroad	440	927	1,303

SOURCE: U.S. Bureau of the Census, Geographic Mobility: March 1996 to March 1997, P20-510, pp. 3-6, table 2.   <www.census.gov/prod/3/98pubs/p20-510u.pdf>, accessed 15 October 1998.

NOTES: 'Total' includes persons of all races/ethnic groups. Persons of Hispanic origin can be of any race. Mobility data from March 1996 to March 1997.

UNITS: Number of persons one year old and over in thousands.

Table 10.13   Projected Fertility Rates, Women 10-49 Years Old, 1997, 2010

	Hispanic women	White women	All women
1997			
Total fertility rate	2,977	1,992	2,063
birth rates			
10-14 years old	2.6	0.8	1.4
15-19 years old	103.7	50.9	59.6
20-24 years old	184.7	109.5	115.9
25-29 years old	152.4	119.0	118.1
30-34 years old	96.7	79.8	78.8
35-39 years old	45.3	31.5	31.6
40-44 years old	10.8	5.4	5.6
45-49 years old	0.6	0.2	0.3
2010			
Total fertility rate	2,777	2,046	2,108
birth rates			
10-14 years old	2.3	0.9	1.6
15-19 years old	95.8	56.0	63.6
20-24 years old	172.6	112.6	118.2
25-29 years old	143.7	120.7	119.5
30-34 years old	91.5	82.0	81.0
35-39 years old	40.5	31.7	32.1
40-44 years old	8.5	5.6	5.9
45-49 years old	0.5	0.2	0.3

SOURCE: U.S. Bureau of the Census, Statistical Abstract of the United States, 1998, p. 79, table 98. C 3.134:998

NOTES: 'All women' includes women of other races and ethnic goups not shown separately. The total fertility rate is the number of births that 1,000 women would have in their lifetime if, at each year of age they experienced the birth rates occurring in the specified year. A total fertility rate of 2,110 represents replacement level fertility for the total population under current mortality conditions (assuming no net immigration). Projections are based on middle fertility assumptions (1.8 births per woman).

UNITS: Total fertility rate and birth rate in births per 1,000 women.

Table 10.14   Selected Characteristics of Persons With a Work Disability, 1997

	Hispanic	White	Total
Persons with a work disability by age			
Total	1,701	13,293	17,439
persons 16-24 years old	180	955	1,390
persons 25-34 years old	278	1,916	2,622
persons 35-44 years old	416	3,024	4,075
persons 45-54 years old	369	3,419	4,368
persons 55-64 years old	457	3,980	4,983
Work disabled as a percent of total population, by age			
Total	9.1%	9.4%	10.2%
persons 16-24 years old	3.8	3.6	4.2
persons 25-34 years old	5.1	5.9	6.5
persons 35-44 years old	9.5	8.3	9.3
persons 45-54 years old	15.0	12.2	13.2
persons 55-64 years old	28.3	21.6	23.1
Percent of work disabled:			
receiving Social Security Income	25.4%	31.6%	30.3%
receiving Food Stamps	35.5	19.9	23.6
covered by Medicaid	48.4	30.4	34.7
residing in public housing	12.2	4.9	7.0
residing in subsidized housing	5.8	2.5	3.4

SOURCE: U.S. Bureau of the Census, Statistical Abstract of the United States, 1998, p. 388, table 622 (data from the Current Population Survey). C 3.134:998

NOTES: 'Total' includes other races and ethnic groups not shown separately. Covers the civilian noninstitutional population and members of the armed forces living off post or with members of their families on post. Persons are classified as having a work disability if they (1) have a health problem or disability which prevents them from or which limits the kind or amount of work they can do; (2) have a service disability or ever retired or left a job for health reasons; (3) did not work in survey reference week or previous year because of long-term illness or disability; or, (4) are under age 65 and are covered by Medicare or receive Supplemental Security Income.

UNITS: Persons with a work disability in thousands of persons; work disabled as a percent of total population in percent; percent of the work disabled by characteristic as a percent of the work disabled.

Table 10.15   Personal Health Practices, 1990

	Hispanic	White	Total
Persons who:			
eat breakfast	52.5%	57.8%	56.4%
rarely snacks	29.3	25.8	25.5
exercised regularly	34.9	41.5	40.7
had 2 or more drinks on any day during the past 2 weeks	4.6	5.8	5.5
are current smokers	23.0	25.6	25.5
are 20% or more above their desireable weight	27.6	26.7	27.5

SOURCE: U.S. Bureau of the Census, <u>Statistical Abstract of the United States, 1994</u>, p. 144, table 215 (data from the National Health Interview Survey). C 3.134:994

NOTES: 'Total' includes other races and ethnic groups not shown separately. Includes persons whose health practices are unknown. Weight data are self-reported.

UNITS: Percent of persons 18 years of age and over.

Table 10.16   Health Care Coverage for Persons Under 65 Years of Age,
by Type of Coverage, 1984 - 1996

	Hispanic	White	Total
1984			
Private insurance	56.3%	79.7%	76.6%
Private insurance obtained through workplace	52.3	71.9	68.9
Medicaid or other public assistance	13.1	5.0	7.3
not covered	29.0	13.3	14.2
1993			
private insurance	48.3%	75.1%	71.3%
private insurance obtained through workplace	44.0	68.8	65.3
Medicaid or public assistance	18.7	8.1	11.1
not covered	32.6	15.6	16.5
1996			
private insurance	47.5%	74.2%	76.6%
private insurance obtained through workplace	43.8	67.6	64.8
Medicaid or other public assistance	20.1	9.3	11.7
not covered	31.6	15.4	16.1

SOURCE: U.S. Department of Health and Human Services, <u>Health United States,</u>
<u>1998</u>, pp. 361-362, table 133 (data from the National Health
Interview Survey). HE 20.6223:98

NOTES: 'Total' includes other races/ethnic groups not shown separately.
Medicaid includes persons receiving AFDC (Aid to Families with
Dependent Children) or SSI (Supplemental Security Income), or
those with a current medicaid card. Not covered includes those
persons not covered by private insurance, Medicaid, Medicare, and
military plans. Data **are** age-adjusted.

UNITS: Percent of the population.

Table 10.17   Health Care Coverage for Persons 65 Years of Age and
Over, by Type of Coverage, 1984 - 1996

	Hispanic	White	Total
1984			
Private insurance	40.5%	76.8%	73.5%
Private insurance obtained through workplace	25.4	40.9	39.1
Medicaid or other public assistance	24.9	5.0	6.9
Medicare only	28.5	16.5	17.7
1993			
Private insurance	39.8%	80.9	77.3%
Private insurance obtained through workplace	18.8	42.7	40.9
Medicaid or other public assistance	31.1	5.6	7.4
Medicare only	26.5	12.4	14.0
1996			
Private insurance	38.6%	75.3%	72.0%
Private insurance obtained through worplace	19.4	39.8	38.6
Medicaid or other public assistance	28.9	6.6	8.3
Medicare only	29.0	16.9	18.1

SOURCE: U.S. Department of Health and Human Services, <u>Health United States, 1998</u>, pp. 363-364, table 134 (data from the National Health Interview Survey). HE 20.6223:98

NOTES: 'Total' includes other races/ethnic groups not shown separately. Medicaid includes persons receiving AFDC (Aid to Families with Dependent Children) or SSI (Supplemental Security Income), or those with a current medicaid card. Not covered includes those persons not covered by private insurance, Medicaid, Medicare, and military plans. Data **are** age-adjusted.

UNITS: Percent of the population.

Table 10.18   Births and Birth Rates, by Age of the Mother, 1997

	Hispanic	White	Total
Live births	701,019	3,094,579	3,903,260
Birth rate per 1,000 population	104.8	64.3	65.4
Birth rate per 1,000 women, by age group			
10-14 years old	2.5	0.7	1.1
15-19 years old	100.1	47.3	53.5
20-24 years old	189.1	107.4	110.9
25-29 years old	163.3	117.0	114.1
30-34 years old	98.8	87.3	84.8
35-39 years old	45.5	36.3	36.0
40-44 years old	10.8	6.8	7.0
45-49 years old	0.6	0.3	0.3

SOURCE: U.S. Department of Health and Human Services, <u>Monthly Vital Statistics Report</u>, Volume 46, No. 12 Supplement 2, September 4, 1998, p. 10, table 2, p. 11, table 3. HE 20.6217:998

NOTES: 'Total' includes other races and ethnic groups not shown separately. Data based on race of the mother.

UNITS: Live births in number of births; rates as shown.

Table 10.19   Birth Rates for Women 15-44 Years of Age, by Live Birth
                    Order, 1997

	Hispanic mothers	White mothers	All mothers
All live births	104.8	64.3	65.4
first births	39.8	26.5	26.8
second births	31.7	21.3	21.2
third births	18.9	10.5	10.6
fourth births and higher	14.4	6.2	6.8

SOURCE: U.S. Department of Health and Human Services, <u>Monthly Vital</u>
            <u>Statistics Report, Volume 46, No. 12 Supplement 2, Semtember 4</u>
            <u>1998</u>, p. 11, table 3. HE 20.6217:998

NOTES: 'All mothers' includes mothers of other races and ethnic groups not
            shown separately. Data based on race of the mother.

UNITS: Live births per 1,000 women 15-44 years of age.

Table 10.20   Death Rates for Malignant Neoplasms of the Breast, for
Females, by Age, 1985 and 1996

	Hispanic women	White women	All Women
1985			
All ages, age adjusted rate	11.8	23.3	23.2
All ages, crude rate	8.8	34.6	32.7
45-54 years old	26.4	46.5	46.7
55-64 years old	43.5	84.2	83.6
65-74 years old	40.9	110.0	107.7
75-84 years old	64.5	140.4	137.7
85 years old and over	85.7	178.9	175.9
1996			
All ages, age adjusted rate	12.8	19.8	20.2
All ages, crude rate	11.4	33.3	31.8
35-44 years old	11.0	12.9	14.2
45-54 years old	27.4	36.9	38.8
55-64 years old	39.7	67.2	67.4
65-74 years old	56.5	99.8	99.1
75-84 years old	85.6	140.6	139.8
85 years old and over	104.5	207.1	204.9

SOURCE: U.S. Department of Health and Human Services, Health United States,
1995 p. 138, table 41; 1998, p. 238, table 42. HE 20.6223:9(year)

NOTES: 'All Women' includes women of other races/ethnic groups not shown separately.
Data excludes deaths of nonresidents of the United States. *Indicates data
based on fewer than 20 deaths.

UNITS: Rate is the number of deaths per 100,000 resident female population, by age group.

Table 10.21   Death Rates for Motor Vehicle Accidents, by Sex and Age, 1993, 1996

	Hispanic		White		Total	
	male	female	male	female	both sexes	
1993						
All ages, age adjusted	25.2	8.2	22.5	9.7	16.0	
All ages, crude	24.7	8.0	22.7	10.3	16.3	
1-14 years old	6.7	4.1	5.9	4.2	5.4	
15-24 years old	43.5	10.5	43.8	17.1	29.1	
25-34 years old	32.8	8.7	29.3	10.2	19.6	
35-44 years old	26.5	8.5	20.9	8.2	14.9	
45-64 years old	23.0	8.5	17.9	8.5	13.5	
65 years old and over	32.0	14.3	30.1	17.0	22.3	

	male	female	male	female	male	female
1996						
All ages, age adjusted	23.2	8.7	22.2	10.4	22.3	10.2
All ages, crude	22.3	8.5	22.4	11.0	22.4	10.7
1-14 years old	5.6	4.7	5.7	4.3	5.9	4.4
15-24 years old	37.5	11.8	42.2	18.1	40.7	17.1
25-34 years old	28.0	9.0	27.0	10.8	27.5	10.7
35-44 years old	23.9	7.7	21.4	9.3	21.8	9.4
45-64 years old	23.8	9.7	19.2	9.3	19.8	9.4
65 years old and over	35.2	13.9	31.1	17.4	31.4	17.2

SOURCE: U.S. Department of Health and Human Services, <u>Health United States, 1998</u>, pp. 246-248, table 46. HE 20.6223:998

NOTES: 'Total' includes other races and ethnic groups not shown separately. Excludes deaths of nonresidents of the United States. *Indicates data based on fewer than 20 deaths.

UNITS: Rate is the number of deaths per 100,000 resident population.

Table 10.22   Death Rates for Homicide and Legal Intervention, by Sex and Age, 1993, 1996

	Hispanic male	Hispanic female	White male	White female	Total both sexes
1993					
All ages, age adjusted	28.4	4.8	8.9	3.0	10.7
All ages, crude	28.9	4.9	8.6	3.0	10.1
15-24 years old	63.9	7.8	17.1	4.2	23.4
25-44 years old	38.6	6.8	12.3	4.2	14.3
45-64 years old	19.7	3.3	6.7	2.2	6.1

	Hispanic male	Hispanic female	White male	White female	Total male	Total female
1996						
All ages, age adjusted	20.4	3.4	7.3	2.5	13.3	3.6
All ages, crude	20.9	3.5	7.0	2.5	12.5	3.5
under 1 year	6.4	7.7	6.5	6.8	8.7	8.9
1-14 years old	2.5	1.5	1.4	1.1	1.9	1.6
15-24 years old	48.9	5.1	14.0	3.3	30.4	5.1
25-44 years old	26.4	4.8	9.9	3.3	17.3	5.0
45-64 years old	13.9	2.7	5.5	2.1	8.0	2.5
65 years old and over	4.0	*	3.2	1.8	4.1	2.1

SOURCE: U.S. Department of Health and Human Services, Health United States, 1998, pp. 250-252, table 47.   HE 20.6223:998

NOTES: 'Total' includes other races/ethnic groups not shown separately. Excludes deaths of nonresidents of the United States. *Based on fewer than 20 deaths.

UNITS: Rate is the number of deaths per 100,000 resident population

Table 10.23   Death Rates for Suicide, by Sex and Age, 1993, 1996

	Hispanic		White		Total	
	male	female	male	female	both sexes	
1993						
All ages, age adjusted	12.6	2.1	19.7	4.6	11.3	
All ages, crude	11.9	2.0	21.4	5.0	12.1	
15-24 years old	18.2	2.9	23.1	4.3	13.5	
25-44 years old	16.6	2.6	25.7	6.3	15.1	
45-64 years old	13.8	2.2	24.6	7.4	14.6	
65 years old and over	22.3	*	40.9	6.1	18.9	
	male	female	male	female	male	female
1996						
All ages, age adjusted	11.1	2.2	19.1	4.4	18.0	4.0
All ages, crude	10.6	2.1	20.9	4.8	19.3	4.4
15-24 years old	15.5	3.3	20.9	3.8	20.0	3.6
25-44 years old	14.6	2.8	25.7	6.4	24.3	5.8
45-64 years old	13.3	2.6	24.9	7.0	23.0	6.4
65 years old and over	17.7	2.5	37.8	5.0	35.2	4.8

SOURCE: U.S. Department of Health and Human Services, Health United States, 1998, pp. 253-255, table 48. HE 20.6223:998

NOTES: 'Total' includes other races and ethnic groups not shown separately. Excludes deaths of nonresidents of the United States. *Indicates data based on fewer than 20 deaths.

UNITS: Rate is the number of deaths per 100,000 resident population.

Table 10.24 Dental Visits by Persons 25 Years Old and Older, by Education, 1990 and 1993

	Hispanic	White	Total
1990			
Total	53.8	64.9	62.3
Education:			
less than 12 years	42.7	41.8	41.2
12 years	59.9	62.8	61.3
13 years or more	67.9	77.3	75.7
1993			
Total	46.2	64.0	60.8
Education:			
less than 12 years	33.0	41.2	38.0
12 years	54.6	60.4	58.7
13 years or more	61.8	75.8	73.8

SOURCE: U.S. Department of Health and Human Services, Health United States, 1995, p. 196, table 81 (data from the National Health Interview Survey). HE 20.6223:95

NOTES: 'Total' includes other races and ethnic groups not shown separately. 'White' excludes white Hispanics. Data excludes residents of U.S. Territories.

UNITS: Percent of the civilian noninstitutionalized population with a dental visit within the past year.

Table 10.25   Hispanic Owned Firms, by Major Industry Group, 1992

	all firms		firms with paid employees			
	firms	sales & receipts	firms	sales & receipts	employees	annual payroll
1992						
All industries	771,708	$72,824,270	115,364	$57,187,370	691,056	$10,768,112
agricultural services, forestry and fishing	31,600	1,464,572	3,985	935,079	19,174	233,781
mining	1,327	304,926	194	250,485	1,527	33,555
construction	97,476	8,212,208	20,192	6,447,317	76,882	1,417,290
manufacturing	18,461	6,157,555	5,209	5,827,194	65,920	1,280,030
transportation and public utilities	47,797	3,702,744	5,100	2,373,189	35,484	606,617
wholesale trade	17,727	12,489,034	5,434	11,687,451	37,547	859,658
retail trade	107,846	17,730,517	27,641	15,116,613	197,626	2,001,152
finance, insurance, and real estate	49,231	4,831,923	5,087	2,774,196	23,177	472,149
services	347,297	16,787,257	40,863	11,558,361	231,977	3,836,093
industries not classified	52,945	1,143,533	1,660	217,485	1,743	27,787

SOURCE: U.S. Bureau of the Census, 1992 Economic Censuses MB92-2 Survey of Minority-Owned Business Enterprises: Hispanic, pp. 13-14, table 1. C 3.258:92-2

NOTES: Data from the 1992 Economic Censuses.

UNITS: Firms in number of firms; sales and receipts in thousands of dollars; employees in number of employees; annual payroll in thousands of dollars.

Table 10.26   Abortions, 1992 - 1995

	Hispanic	White	All Races
1992	30.7	23.6	33.5
1993	28.9	23.1	33.4
1994	27.8	21.7	32.1
1995	26.5	20.4	31.1

SOURCE: U.S. Department of Health and Human Services, <u>Health, United States, 1998</u> , p. 185, table 15. HE 20.6223:998

NOTES: 'All Races' includes women of other races not shown separately.
"White" includes women of Hispanic ethnicity.

UNITS: Abortions per 100 live births.

Glossary

ACUTE CONDITION see **CONDITION (HEALTH).**

AGE ADJUSTMENT

Age adjustment, using the direct method, is the application of the age specific rates in a population of interest to a standardized age distribution in order to eliminate the differences in observed rates that result from age differences in population composition. This adjustment is usually done when comparing two or more populations at one point in time, or one population at two or more points in time.

AGGRAVATED ASSAULT see **CRIME.**

ARSON see **CRIME.**

AVERAGE see **MEAN; MEDIAN.**

BED (HOSPITAL; NURSING HOME)

Any bed that is staffed for use by inpatients is counted as a bed in a facility.

BED-DISABILITY DAY see **DISABILITY DAY.**

BIRTH see **LIVE BIRTH.**

BURGLARY see **CRIME.**

CAUSE OF DEATH

For the purpose of national mortality statistics, every death is attributed to one underlying condition, based on information reported on the death certificate and utilizing the international rules (International Classifications of Disease) for selecting the underlying cause of death from reported conditions. Selected causes of death are shown on tables.

CHRONIC CONDITION see **CONDITION (HEALTH).**

CIVILIAN LABOR FORCE

All persons (excluding members of the Armed Forces) who are either employed or unemployed. (The experienced civilian labor force is a subgroup of the civilian labor force, composed of all persons, employed and unemployed, that have worked before.)

Employed persons are those persons 16 years old and over who were either a) "at work"- those who did any work at all as paid employees, or in their own business or profession, or on their own farm, or worked 15 or more hours as unpaid workers on a family farm or in a family business; or b) "with a job but not at work"- those who did not work during the reference period but had jobs or businesses from which they were temporarily absent due to illness, bad weather, industrial dispute, vacation, or other personal reasons. Excluded from the employed are persons whose only activity consisted of work around the house or volunteer work for religious, charitable, and similar organizations.

Employed persons are classified as either **full-time workers**, those who worked 35 hours or more per week; or **part-time workers**, those who worked less than 35 hours per week.

Unemployed persons are those who were neither "at work" nor "with a job, but not at work" and who were a) looking for work, and b) available to accept a job. Also included as unemployed are persons who are waiting to be called back to a job from which they have been laid off. The unemployed are divided into four groups according to reason for unemployment:

--**job losers** (including those who have been laid off)
--**job leavers** who have left their job voluntarily
--**reentrants**, persons who have worked before and are reentering the labor force
--**new entrants** to the labor force looking for work

CIVILIAN NONINSTITUTIONAL POPULATION see **POPULATION**.

CIVILIAN POPULATION see **POPULATION**.

COLLEGE

A postsecondary school which offers a general or liberal arts education, usually leading to an associate, bachelor's, master's, doctor's, or first professional degree. Junior colleges and community colleges are included. See also **Institution of Higher Education; University**.

COMMUNITY HOSPITAL

All non-federal short term hospitals, excluding hospital units of institutions, whose services are available to the public. **Short term hospitals** are those where the average length of stay is less than 30 days.

CONDITION (HEALTH)

A health condition is a departure from a state of physical or mental well-being. Based on duration, there are two categories of conditions: acute and chronic.

An **acute condition** is one that has lasted less than three months, and has involved either a physician visit (medical attention) or restricted activity.

A **chronic condition** is any condition lasting three months or more, or is one classified as chronic regardless of the time of onset. See also **Health Limitation of Activity**.

CONSOLIDATED METROPOLITAN STATISTICAL AREA (CMSA)

A geographic area concept introduced in June, 1984, which, in combination with Metropolitan Statistical Area (MSA), and Primary Metropolitan Statistical Area (PMSA), replace the Standard Metropolitan Statistical Area (SMSA) concept. CMSAs are designated in accordance with criteria established by the federal Office of Management and Budget (OMB). In general CMSAs are MSAs with a population of one million or more, and which have component PMSAs. See also **Metropolitan Statistical Area.**

CONSUMER EXPENDITURE SURVEY

A survey of current consumer expenditures reflecting the buying habits of American consumers. Begun in 1979 and conducted jointly by the U.S. Bureau of Labor Statistics and the U.S. Bureau of the Census, the survey consists of two parts: an interview panel survey in which the expenditures of consumer units are obtained in five interviews conducted every three months, and a diary or recordkeeping survey completed by the participating households for two consecutive one-week periods. See also **Consumer Unit.**

The Consumer Expenditure Survey, which collects data on expenditures, should not be confused with the Consumer Price Index, which measures the average change in prices of consumer goods and services.

CONSUMER UNIT

An entity used as the basis of the Consumer Expenditure Survey. A consumer unit comprises either

--all the members of a particular household who are related by blood, marriage, adoption, or other legal arrangements; or

--a person living alone or sharing a household with others, or living as a roomer in a private home or lodging house or in a permanent living quarters in a hotel or motel, but who is financially independent; or

--two or more persons living together who pool their income to make joint expenditure decisions.

A consumer unit may or may not be a household.

CRIME

A crime is an action which is prohibited by law. Their are two major statistical programs which measure crime in the United States. The first is the Uniform Crime Reporting (UCR) program, administered by the FBI. The Bureau receives monthly and annual reports from most police agencies around the country (covering approximately 97% of the population). These reports contain information on eight major types of crime (called collectively, serious crime), which are known to police. Serious crime consists of four violent crimes (murder and non-negligent manslaughter, which includes willful felonious homicides and is based on police investigations rather than determinations of a medical examiner; forcible rape, which includes attempted rape; robbery, which includes stealing or taking anything of value by force or violence, or by threat of force or violence, and includes attempted robbery; and aggravated assault which includes intent to kill), and four property crimes (burglary, which includes any unlawful entry to commit a felony or theft and includes attempted burglary and burglary followed by larceny; larceny, which includes theft of property or articles of value without use of force, violence, or fraud, and excludes embezzlement, con games, forgery, etc.; motor vehicle theft, which includes all cases where vehicles are driven away and abandoned, but excludes vehicles taken for temporary use and returned by the taker; and arson, which includes any willful or malicious burning or attempt to burn, with or without the intent to defraud, of a dwelling house, public building, motor vehicle, aircraft, or personal property of another.)

The second approach to the measurement of crime is through the National Crime Survey (NCS) administered by the Bureau of Justice Statistics. The survey is based on a representative sample of approximately 49,000 households, inhabited by about 102,000 persons age 12 and over. Although the categories of crime are similar to those used by the FBI in the UCR, the NCS is based on reports of victimization directly by victims, as opposed to crimes reported to police as in the UCR. As might be imagined, not all crimes are reported or known to police, therefore NCS estimates of crime tend to be significantly higher than UCR figures. The NCS also differs from the UCR in that only crimes whose victims can be interviewed are included (hence there are no homicide statistics), and only victims who are 12 years old or older are counted. The two central concepts in the NCS are victimization, which is the specific criminal act as it affects a single victim, and a criminal incident, which is a specific criminal act involving one or more victims. Thus in regard to personal crime, there are more victimizations, than incidents.

DEATH see CAUSE OF DEATH; INFANT MORTALITY.

DISABILITY

The presence of a physical, mental, or other health condition which has lasted six or more months and which limits or prevents a particular type of activity. See also **Work Disability.**

DISABILITY DAY

A day on which a person's usual activity is reduced because of illness or injury. There are four types of disability days (which are not mutually exclusive). They are

--a **restricted-activity day,** a day on which a person cuts down on his or her usual activities because of illness or an injury.

--a **bed-disability day,** a day on which a person stays in bed more than half of the daylight hours (or normal waking hours) because of a specific illness or injury. All hospital days are bed-disability days. Bed disability days may also be work-loss days or school loss days.

--a **work-loss day,** a day on which a person did not work at his or her job or business for at least half of his or her normal workday because of a specific illness or injury. Work loss days are determined only for employed persons.

--a **school-loss day,** a day on which a child did not attend school for at least half of his or her normal schoolday because of a specific illness or injury. School-loss days are determined only for children 6 to 16 years of age.

DISPOSABLE INCOME see INCOME.

EMPLOYED PERSONS see CIVILIAN LABOR FORCE.

EMPLOYMENT STATUS see **LABOR FORCE STATUS.**

ENROLLMENT
> The total number of students registered in a given school unit at a given time, generally in the fall of the year. See also **Full-Time Enrollment; Part-Time Enrollment.**

EVER MARRIED PERSONS see **MARITAL STATUS.**

EXPERIENCED CIVILIAN LABOR FORCE
> That portion of the Civilian Labor Force, both employed and unemployed, that have worked before. Excludes new entrants to the Civilian Labor Force. See also **Civilian Labor Force.**

EXPERIENCED WORKER see **EXPERIENCED CIVILIAN LABOR FORCE.**

FAMILY
> A type (subgroup) of household in which there are two or more persons living together (including the householder) who are related by birth, marriage, or adoption. All such related persons in one housing unit are considered as members of one family. (For example, if the son or daughter of the family householder and that son's or daughter's spouse and/or children are members of the household, they are all counted as part of the householder's family.) However, non-family members who are not related to the householder (such as a roomer or boarder and his or her spouse, or a resident employee and his or her spouse who are living in), are not counted as family members but as unrelated individuals living in a family household. Thus for Census purposes, a housing unit can contain only one household, and a household can contain only one family. See also **Family Type; Household; Householder; Unrelated Individual.**

FAMILY INCOME see **INCOME.**

FAMILY TYPE
> Families are classified by type according to the sex of the householder and the presence of a spouse and children. The three main types of households are: **Married Couples,** in which a husband and wife live together (with or without other persons in the household); **Male Householder, No Wife Present,** in which a male householder lives together with other members of his family but without a wife; and **Female Householder, No Husband Present,** in which a female householder lives together with other members of her family but without a husband. See also **Family; Family Household; Household.**

FARM
> As defined by the Bureau of the Census (and adopted by the Department of Agriculture), a farm is any place from which $1,000 or more of agricultural products were sold, or would have been sold during a given year. Control of the farm may be exercised through ownership or management, or through a lease, rental or cropping

arrangement. In the case of landowners who have one or more tenants or renters, the land operated by each is counted as a separate farm. This definition has been in effect since 1974.

FARMLAND

All land under the control of a farm operator, including land not actually under cultivation or not used for pasture or grazing. Rent free land is included as part of a farm only if the operator has sole use of it. Land used for pasture or grazing on a per head basis that is neither owned nor leased by the farm operator is not included except for grazing lands controlled by grazing associations leased on a per acre basis.

FARM INCOME

Gross farm income comprises cash receipts from farm marketings of crops and livestock, federal government payments made directly to farmers for farm-related activities, rental value of farm homes, value of farm products consumed in farm homes, and other farm-related income such as machine hire and custom work.

FULL-TIME ENROLLMENT (HIGHER EDUCATION)

The number of students enrolled in higher education courses with a total credit load equal to at least 75% of the normal full-time course load.

FULL-TIME WORKERS see CIVILIAN LABOR FORCE.

HEALTH LIMITATION OF ACTIVITY

A characteristic of persons with chronic conditions. Each person identified as having a chronic condition is classified as to the extent to which his or her activities are limited by the condition as follows:

--persons unable to carry on a major activity (that is the principal activity of a person of his or her age-sex group: for persons 1-5 years of age, it refers to ordinary play with other children; for persons 6-16 years of age, it refers to school attendance; for persons 17 years of age and over, it usually refers to a job, housework, or school attendance.)

--persons limited in the amount or kind of major activity performed.

--persons not limited in major activity, but otherwise limited.

--persons not limited in activity.

See also **Condition (Health).**

HEALTH MAINTENANCE ORGANIZATION (HMO)

A prepaid health plan delivering comprehensive care to members through designated providers, having a fixed monthly payment for health care services, and requiring members to be in the plan for a specified period of time (usually one year). HMOs are distinguished by the relationship of the providers to the plan. HMO model types are: **Group** -- an HMO that delivers health services through a physician group controlled by the HMO, or an HMO that contracts with one or more independent group practices to provide health services; **Individual Practice Association (IPA)** -- an HMO that contracts directly with physicians in independent practice, and/or contracts with one or more associations of physicians in independent practice, and/or contracts with one or more multispecialty group practices (but the plan is predominantly organized around solo-single specialty practices).

HIGHER EDUCATION see **INSTITUTION OF HIGHER EDUCATION.**

HISPANIC ORIGIN

An aspect of a person's ancestry. The Bureau of the Census in many of its survey asks persons if they are of Hispanic origin. There are four main subcategories of Hispanic origin: Mexican, Puerto Rican, Cuban, and other Hispanic. Hispanic origin is not a racial classification. Persons may be of any race and of Hispanic origin. Hispanic origin is used interchangeably with Spanish and Spanish origin.

HOME OWNERSHIP see **TENURE.**

HOSPITAL see **COMMUNITY HOSPITAL.**

HOSPITAL DAY

A hospital day is a night spent in a hospital by a person admitted as an inpatient.

HOUSEHOLD

The person or persons occupying a housing unit. There are two main types of households: family households, which consist of two or more persons related by birth, marriage, or adoption living together (see also **Family; Family Type**); and non-family households, which consist of a person living alone, or together with unrelated individuals (see Unrelated Individuals). See also **Householder.**

HOUSEHOLD INCOME see **INCOME.**

HOUSEHOLD TYPE see **HOUSEHOLD.**

HOUSEHOLDER

The person in whose name a housing unit is rented or owned.

HOUSING UNIT

A house, apartment, mobile home or trailer, group of rooms, or single room occupied as a separate living quarter, or, if vacant, intended for occupancy as a separate living quarter. Separate living quarters are those in which the occupants live and eat separately from any other persons in the building and which have direct access from the outside of the building or through a common hall.

Both occupied and vacant housing units are counted in many surveys; however, recreational vehicles, boats, caves, tents, railroad cars, and the like are only included if they are occupied as someone's usual place of residence. Vacant mobile homes are included if they are intended for occupancy on the site where they stand. Vacant mobile homes on dealer's sales lots, at the factory, or in storage yards are excluded.

Most housing unit data is for year-round housing units which comprises all occupied housing units plus vacant housing units intended for year round use. Vacant units held for seasonal use or migratory labor are excluded. See also **Occupancy Status, Rooms, Specified Owner-Occupied Housing Units, Tenure, Value (Housing).**

HOUSING TENURE see **TENURE.**

INCIDENT see **CRIME.**

INCOME

The term income has different definitions depending on how it is modified and in what situation it is used. Like many government statistical terms, income can be viewed hierarchically.

Personal income is the current income received by persons from all sources, minus their personal contributions for social insurance. Persons include individuals (including owners of unincorporated firms), non-profit institutions serving individuals, private trust funds, and private non-insured welfare funds. Personal income includes transfers (payments not resulting from current production) from government and business such as Social Security benefits, public assistance, etc., but excludes transfers among persons. Also included are certain non-monetary types of income, chiefly estimated net rental value to owner-occupants of their homes, the value of services furnished without payment by financial intermediaries, and food and fuel produced and consumed on farms.

Disposable personal income is personal income less personal tax and non-tax payments. It is income available to persons for spending and saving. Personal tax and non-tax payments are tax payments (net of refunds) by persons (excluding contributions for social insurance) that are not chargeable to business expenses, and certain personal payments to general government that are treated like taxes. Personal taxes include income, estate and gift, personal property, and motor vehicle licenses. Non-tax payments include passport fees, fines and penalties, donations, tuition and fees paid to schools and hospitals mainly operated by the government.

Money income is a smaller less inclusive category than personal income. Money income is the sum of the amounts received from wages and salaries, self-employment income (including losses), Social Security, Supplemental Security Income, public assistance, interest, dividends, rents, royalties, estate or trust income, veterans payments, unemployment and workers' compensation payments, private and government retirement and disability pensions, alimony, child support, and any other source of money income which was regularly received. Capital gains or losses and lump-sum or one-time payments, such as life insurance settlements, are excluded. Also excluded are non-cash benefits such as food stamps, health benefits, housing subsidies, rent-free housing, and the goods produced and consumed on farms. Money income is reported for households and various household types as well as for unrelated individuals. (In regard to family money income it should be noted that only the amount received by all family members 15 years old and over is counted, and excludes income received by household members not related to the householder.) It is reported in aggregate, median, mean, and per capita amounts. Money income is also used for determining the poverty status of families and unrelated individuals.

INFANT MORTALITY
The deaths of live-born children who do not reach their first birthday. Infant mortality is usually expressed as a rate per 1,000 live births.

INPATIENT DAYS (HOSPITALS)
The number of adult and pediatric days of care rendered during a given period. See also Hospital Day.

INSTITUTION OF HIGHER EDUCATION
An institution which offers programs of study beyond the secondary school level terminating in an associate, baccalaureate, or higher degree. See also **College; University.**

JAIL
A facility, usually operated by a local law enforcement agency, holding persons detained pending adjudication and/or persons committed after adjudication to a sentence of one year or less.

LABOR FORCE STATUS
A term which refers to whether or not a person is in the labor force, and, if in the labor force, whether he or she is employed or unemployed, a full-time worker or a part-time worker, etc. Persons are in the labor force if they are in the civilian labor force or in the Armed Forces.

The civilian labor force consists of both employed and unemployed persons, full-time and part-time workers. Generally, persons outside the labor force consist of full-time homemakers, students who do not work, retired persons, and inmates of institutions. "Discouraged workers," those who do not have a job and have not been seeking one, are also considered to be not in the labor force. See also **Civilian Labor Force.**

LARCENY see **CRIME.**

LIMITATION OF ACTIVITY see **HEALTH LIMITATION OF ACTIVITY**.

LIVE BIRTH
The live birth of an infant, defined as the complete expulsion or extraction from its mother of a product of conception, irrespective of the duration of the pregnancy, which, after such separation, breathes or shows any evidence of life such as heartbeat, umbilical cord pulsation, or definite movement of voluntary muscles, whether or not the umbilical cord has been cut or the placenta is attached. Each such birth is considered live born.

MARITAL STATUS

All persons 15 years of age and older are classified by the Bureau of the Census according to marital status. The Bureau defines two broad categories of marital status: **Single** - all those persons who have never been married (including persons whose marriage has been annulled), and **Ever married** - which is composed of the now married, the widowed, and the divorced. **Now married** persons are those who are legally married (as well as some persons who have common law marriages, along with some unmarried couples who live together and report their marital status as married), and whose marriage has not ended by widowhood or divorce. The now married are sometimes further subdivided: married, spouse present; separated; married, spouse absent; married, spouse absent, other. **Married, spouse present** covers married couples living together. **Separated** includes those persons legally separated or otherwise absent from their spouse because of marital discord (such as persons who have been deserted or who have parted because they no longer want to live together but who have not obtained a divorce). Separated includes persons with a limited divorce. **Married, spouse absent** covers those households where the both the husband and the wife were not counted as members of the same household, (or where both husband and wife lived together in group quarters). **Married, spouse absent, other**, includes those married persons whose spouse was not counted as a member of the same household, besides those who are separated. Included are persons whose spouse was employed and living away from home, absent in the armed forces, or was an inmate of an institution. **Widowed** includes widows and widowers who have not remarried. **Divorced** includes persons who are legally divorced and have not remarried.

MARRIED COUPLES see FAMILY TYPE.

MARRIED PERSONS see MARITAL STATUS.

MEAN

The arithmetic average of a set of values. It is derived by dividing the sum of a group of numerical items by the total number of items. Mean income (of a population), for example, is defined as the value obtained by dividing the total or aggregate income by the population. Thus, the mean income for families is obtained by dividing the aggregate of all income reported by persons in families by the total number of families. See also **Median.**

MEDIAN

In general, a value that divides the total range of values into two equal parts. For example, to say that the median money income of families in the United States in 1985 was $27,735 indicates that half of all families had incomes larger than that value, and half had less. See also **Mean.**

MEDICAID

A federally funded but state administered and operated program which provides medical benefits to certain low income persons in need of medical care. The program, authorized in 1965 by Title XIX of the Social Security Act, categorically covers participants in the Aid to Families with Dependent Children (AFDC) program, as well as some participants in the Supplemental Security Income (SSI) program, along with those other people deemed medically needy in each participating state. Each state determines the benefits covered, rates of payment to providers, and methods of administering the program.

MEDICARE

A federally funded nationwide health insurance program providing health insurance protection to people 65 years of age and over, people eligible for social security disability payments for more than two years, and people with end-state renal disease, regardless of income. The program was enacted July 30, 1965, as title XVIII, Health Insurance for the Aged, of the Social Security Act, and became effective on July 1, 1966. It consists of two separate but coordinated programs: hospital insurance (Part A), and supplementary medical insurance (Part B).

METROPOLITAN AREA see CONSOLIDATED METROPOLITAN STATISTICAL AREA; METROPOLITAN STATISTICAL AREA; PRIMARY METROPOLITAN STATISTICAL AREA; STANDARD CONSOLIDATED STATISTICAL AREA; STANDARD METROPOLITAN STATISTICAL AREA

METROPOLITAN STATISTICAL AREA (MSA)

A geographic concept introduced in June, 1984, to replace the Standard Metropolitan Statistical Area (SMSA). In general, an MSA is a geographic area consisting of a large population nucleus, together with adjacent communities that have a high degree of economic and social integration with that nucleus. MSAs are designated in accordance with a detailed 16 section criteria established by the federal Office of Management and Budget (OMB). In general, MSAs are a county based concept which must include a city that, with contiguous, densely settled territory, constitutes a Census Bureau defined urbanized area having at least 50,000 population. (However, if an MSA's largest city has less than 50,000 population, the MSA as a whole must have a total population of at least 100,000). Adjacent MSAs are consolidated into a single MSA if certain conditions relating to commuting to work, size, and geographic proximity are met. See also **Consolidated Metropolitan Statistical Area; New England County Metropolitan Area; Primary Metropolitan Statistical Area.**

NEW ENGLAND COUNTY METROPOLITAN AREA (NECMA)

A geographic concept developed for the New England states (Massachusetts, Connecticut, Rhode Island, Maine, New Hampshire, Vermont) to present data that is only available on a county-level basis . Unlike the rest of the country, Metropolitan Statistical Areas (MSAs) in the New England states are officially defined in terms of cities and towns instead of counties. As a result New England MSA data may not be directly comparable to MSA data in the rest of the country. NECMAs are county-based geographic areas (which follow the same general guidelines of MSAs in other parts of the country) and thus provide a basis of comparison with other states. NECMAs do not replace the MSAs in New England, but supplement them.

MOBILE HOME see **HOUSING UNIT.**

MONEY INCOME see **INCOME.**

MURDER see **CRIME.**

NATIONAL CRIME SURVEY

A twice yearly survey of 49,000 households comprising over 102,000 inhabitants 12 years of age and older. Administered by the Bureau of Justice Statistics, the survey measures criminal victimization by surveying victims directly. It differs from the FBI Uniform Crime Report (UCR) which is based on crimes reported to police. See also **Crime.**

NURSING HOME

A facility with three or more beds providing adults with nursing care and/or personal care (such as help with bathing, eating, using toilet facilities, or dressing) and/or supervision over such activities as money management, walking, and shopping.

OCCUPANCY STATUS (HOUSING)

The classification of all housing units as either occupied or vacant. **Occupied housing units** are those that have one or more persons living in them as their usual residence, and include units whose usual occupants are temporarily absent (e.g., on vacation). **Vacant housing units** are those that have no one living in them as their usual residence. Also classified as vacant are housing units that are temporarily occupied solely by persons who have a usual residence elsewhere, newly constructed units completed to the point where all exterior windows and doors are installed and final usable floors are in place, and vacant mobile homes or trailers intended to be occupied on the site on which they stand.

OCCUPATION

The kind of work a person does at a job or business. Occupation is reported for a given survey period, (most frequently the period covered by the survey, the reference period, is the week including March 12). If the person was not at work during the reference period, occupation usually refers to the person's most recent job or business. Persons working at more than one job are asked to identify the job at which he or she works the most hours, which is then counted as his or her occupation.

Occupations are classified according to the Standard Occupational Classification system (SOC), a system promulgated by the federal Office of Management and Budget.

OWNER OCCUPIED HOUSING UNIT see **TENURE.**

PART-TIME ENROLLMENT (HIGHER EDUCATION)

The number of students enrolled in higher education courses with a total credit load of less than 75% of the normal full-time credit load.

PART-TIME WORKERS see CIVILIAN LABOR FORCE.

PERSONAL INCOME see INCOME.

POPULATION

The number of inhabitants of an area. The total population of the United States is the sum of all persons living within the United States, plus all members of the Armed Forces living in foreign countries, Puerto Rico, Guam, and the U.S. Virgin Islands. Other Americans living abroad (e.g., civilian federal employees and dependents of members of the Armed Forces or other federal employees are not included).

The **resident population of the United States**, is the population living within the geographic United States. This includes members of the Armed Forces stationed in the United States and their families as well as foreigners working or studying here. It excludes foreign military, naval, and diplomatic personnel and their families located here and residing in embassies or similar quarters, as well as Americans living abroad. Resident population is often the denominator when calculating birth and death rates, incidence of disease, and other rates.

The **civilian population** is the resident population excluding members of the Armed Forces. However, families of members of the Armed Forces are included.

The **civilian non-institutional population** is the civilian population not residing in institutions. Institutions include, correctional institutions; detention homes and training schools for juvenile delinquents; homes for the aged and dependent (e.g., nursing homes and convalescent homes); homes for dependent and neglected children; homes and schools for the mentally and physically handicapped; homes for unwed mothers; psychiatric, tuberculosis, and chronic disease hospitals; and residential treatment centers.

POVERTY STATUS

Although the term poverty connotes a complex set of economic, social, and psychological conditions, the standard statistical definition provides for only estimates of economic poverty. These are based on the receipt of money income before taxes and exclude the value of government payments and transfers such as food stamps or Medicare; private transfers, such as health insurance premiums paid by employers; gifts; the depletion of assets; and borrowed money. Thus the term poverty as used by government agencies, classifies persons and families in relation to being above or below a specified income level, or poverty threshold. Those below this threshold are said to be in poverty, or more accurately, as below the poverty level. Poverty thresholds vary by size of family, number of children, and age of householder and are updated annually. Poverty status is also determined for unrelated individuals living in households, but not for those living in group quarters nor for persons in the Armed Forces. The poverty threshold is revised each year according to formula based on the Consumer Price Index.

PRIMARY METROPOLITAN STATISTICAL AREA (PMSA)

This geographic concept, introduced in June, 1984, combines with Metropolitan Statistical Area (MSA) and Consolidated Metropolitan Statistical Areas (CMSA), to replace the Standard Metropolitan Statistical Area (SMSA) concept. PMSAs are designated according to criteria established by the federal Office of Management and Budget. In general PMSAs are those counties with populations of at least 100,000 (60% must be urban), in which less than 50% of its resident workers commute to jobs outside the county. PMSAs are parts of Consolidated Metropolitan Statistical Areas (CMSAs).

PRISON

A confinement facility having custodial authority over adults sentenced to confinement for a period of more than one year. Prisons are usually run by State or federal authorities.

PRIVATE SCHOOL see SCHOOL.

PROPERTY CRIME see CRIME.

PUBLIC SCHOOL see SCHOOL.

RACE

The Bureau of the Census in many of its surveys (most notably in the decennial censuses of population) asks all persons to identify themselves according to race. The concept of race as used by the Bureau reflects the self-identification of the respondents. It is not meant to denote any clear cut scientific or biological definition.

Although it is often reported with racial categories, **Hispanic origin**, or Spanish origin, is not a racial category. Persons may be of any race and of Hispanic origin. Those who describe themselves as Hispanic (or Mexican, Cuban, Chicano, etc.) in response to a question about race, are included by the Bureau in the racial classification, "other." See also **Hispanic Origin.**

RAPE see CRIME.

REFERENCE PERSON

Most frequently, the person who responds to a government survey. Most surveys done by the federal government are based on households and begin by asking the initial respondent the name of the person in whose name the housing unit is owned or rented (this person is designated as the householder). Usually the householder is the reference person. Other household members are defined in relation to the householder.

REGION

The Bureau of the Census has divided the United States into four regions. This division is the primary geographic subdivision of the nation for statistical reporting purposes. As a result, almost all federal agencies, along with many private data collectors, have adopted the regional subdivision and use it for presenting statistical data.

The four regions are the **Northeast** (Maine, New Hampshire, Vermont, Massachusetts, Rhode Island, Connecticut, New York, New Jersey, Pennsylvania); the **Midwest** (Ohio, Indiana, Illinois, Michigan, Wisconsin, Minnesota, Iowa, Missouri, North Dakota, South Dakota, Kansas, Nebraska); the **South** (Delaware, Maryland, District of Columbia, Virginia, West Virginia, North Carolina, South Carolina, Georgia, Florida, Kentucky, Tennessee, Alabama, Mississippi, Arkansas, Louisiana, Oklahoma, Texas); and the **West** (Montana, Idaho, Colorado, Wyoming, New Mexico, Arizona, Utah, Nevada, Washington, Oregon, California, Alaska, Hawaii). In this book, all regional data conform to this definition.

REGULAR SCHOOL see **SCHOOL**.

RENTER OCCUPIED HOUSING UNIT see **TENURE**.

RESIDENT POPULATION see **POPULATION**.

RESTRICTED-ACTIVITY DAY see **DISABILITY DAY**.

ROBBERY see **CRIME**.

ROOMS (HOUSING)

The number of whole rooms intended for living purposes in both occupied and vacant housing units. These rooms include living rooms, dining rooms, kitchens, bedrooms, finished recreation rooms, enclosed porches suitable for year-round use, and lodger's rooms. Excluded are strip or Pullman kitchens, bathrooms, open porches, balconies, foyers, halls, half-rooms, utility rooms, unfinished attics or basements, or other space used for storage. A partially divided room, such as a dinette next to a kitchen or living room, is a separate room only if there is a partition from floor to ceiling, but not if the partition consists solely of shelves or cabinets.

RURAL see **URBAN/RURAL POPULATION**.

SCHOOL

Elementary and secondary schools are divisions of the school system consisting of students in one or more grade groups or other identifiable groups, organized as one unit with one or more teachers giving instruction of a defined type, and housed in a school plant of one or more buildings. More than one school may be housed in one school plant as is the case where elementary and secondary programs are housed in the same building.

Regular schools generally are those which advance a person toward a diploma or degree. They include public and private nursery schools, kindergartens, graded schools, colleges, universities, and professional schools.

Public schools are controlled and supported by local, state, or federal government agencies.

Private schools are controlled and supported mainly by religious organizations, private persons, or private organizations.

SCHOOL ENROLLMENT see **ENROLLMENT**.

SCHOOL-LOSS DAY see **DISABILITY DAY**.

SELF-EMPLOYMENT INCOME
 A type of money income which comprises net income (gross receipts minus operating expenses) received by persons from an unincorporated business, profession, and/or from the operation of a farm as a farm owner, tenant, or sharecropper. See also **Money Income**.

SEPARATED PERSONS see **MARITAL STATUS**.

SERIOUS CRIME see **CRIME**.

SINGLE PERSON HOUSEHOLDS see **HOUSEHOLD**.

SINGLE PERSONS see **MARITAL STATUS**.

SPECIFIED OWNER-OCCUPIED HOUSING UNITS
 Specified owner-occupied units are single family houses on less than ten acres, which have no commercial enterprise or medical practice on the property. Excluded are owner-occupied condominium housing units, mobile homes, trailers, boats, tents, or vans occupied as a usual residence as well as owner-occupied non-condominium units in multi-family buildings. See also **Housing Unit.**

STANDARD CONSOLIDATED STATISTICAL AREA (SCSA)
 A large concentration of metropolitan population composed of two or more contiguous Standard Metropolitan Statistical Areas (SMSAs) which together meet certain criteria of population size, urban character, social and economic integration, and/or contiguity of urbanized areas. Each SCSA must have a population of one million or more. The SCSA concept was replaced with the new metropolitan area classifications in June, 1984. See Consolidated Metropolitan Statistical Area; Metropolitan Statistical Area; Primary Metropolitan Statistical Area.

STANDARD METROPOLITAN STATISTICAL AREA (SMSA)
 A geographic area concept used until 1984. In general, an SMSA is a large population nucleus and nearby communities which have a high degree of economic and social integration within that nucleus. Each SMSA consists of one or more entire counties (or county equivalents) that meet certain criteria of population, commuting ties, and metropolitan character. In New England, towns and cities rather than counties are the basic units and count as county equivalents. An SMSA includes a city and, generally, the entire surrounding urbanized area and the remainder of the county or counties in which the urbanized area is located. An SMSA also includes those additional outlying counties which meet specified criteria relating to metropolitan character and level of commuting ties.

The SMSA concept was developed in 1949 and has been refined for each succeeding decennial census since 1950. In June, 1984, SMSAs were superseded by three new metropolitan area concepts: Metropolitan Statistical Areas (MSAs), Consolidated Metropolitan Statistical Areas (CMSAs), and Primary Metropolitan Statistical Areas (PMSAs).

TAXES

Compulsory contributions exacted by a government for public purposes (except employee and employer assessments for retirement and social insurance purposes, which are classified as insurance trust revenue). All tax revenue is classified as general revenue and comprises amounts received (including interest and penalties, but excluding protested amounts and refunds) from all taxes imposed by a government.

TENURE

A concept relating to housing units. All occupied housing units are classified as being either owner-occupied or renter occupied. A housing unit is owner-occupied if the owner or co-owner lives in the unit even if the unit is mortgaged or not fully paid for. All other housing units are considered to be renter occupied, regardless of whether or not cash rent is paid for them by a member of the household. See also **Housing Unit.**

UNEMPLOYED PERSONS see CIVILIAN LABOR FORCE.

UNEMPLOYMENT see CIVILIAN LABOR FORCE.

UNIFORM CRIME REPORTING (UCR) PROGRAM

A program administered by the FBI which collects reports from most police agencies in the nation (covering approximately 95% of the population) on serious crimes known to police (violent crime and property crime), arrests, police officers and related items. The Bureau issues monthly and annual summary reports based on the program. See also **Crime.**

UNIVERSITY

An institution of higher education consisting of a liberal arts college, a diverse graduate program, and usually two or more professional schools or faculties and empowered to confer degrees in various fields of study. See also **Higher Education.**

UNRELATED INDIVIDUAL

An unrelated individual is generally a person living in a household, and is either: 1) a householder living alone or only with persons who are not related to him or her by blood, marriage, or adoption, or; 2) a roomer, boarder, partner, roommate, or resident employee unrelated to the householder. Certain persons living in group quarters (who are not inmates of institutions) are also counted as unrelated individuals.

URBAN/RURAL POPULATION

Urban and rural are type of area concepts rather than specific areas outlined on maps. The urban population comprises all persons living in urbanized areas and in places of 2,500 or more inhabitants outside urbanized areas. The rural population consists of everyone else. Therefore, a rural classification need not imply a farm or sparsely settled areas, since a small city or town is rural when it is outside an urbanized area and has fewer than 2,500 inhabitants. The terms urban and rural are independent of metropolitan and non-metropolitan; both urban and rural areas occur inside and outside metropolitan areas. See also **Urbanized Area.**

URBANIZED AREA

A population concentration of at least 50,000 inhabitants, generally consisting of a central city and the surrounding, closely settled, contiguous territory (suburbs). The urbanized area criteria define a boundary based on a population density of at least 1,000 persons per square mile, but also include some less densely settled areas, such as industrial parks and railroad yards, if they are within areas of dense urban development. The density level of 1,000 persons per square mile corresponds approximately to the contiguously built-up area around a city or cities. The urban fringe is that part of the urbanized area outside of a central city or cities.

Typically, an entire urbanized area is included within an Standard Metropolitan Statistical Area (SMSA) or Metropolitan Statistical Area (MSA). The SMSA (or MSA) is usually much larger in terms of area and includes territory where the population density is less than 1,000. Occasionally more than one urbanized area is located within an SMSA (MSA). In some cases a small part of an urbanized area may extend beyond an SMSA (MSA) boundary, or possibly into an adjacent SMSA (MSA). Urbanized areas sometimes cross state boundaries as well.

VACANCY STATUS see OCCUPANCY STATUS.

VALUE (HOUSING UNITS)

In surveys done by the Bureau of the Census, the value of owner-occupied housing units is the respondent's estimate of the current dollar worth of the property; for vacant units, the value is the price asked for the property. A property is defined as the house and the land on which it stands. Respondents are asked by the Bureau to estimate the value of the house and land even if they own only the house, or own the house jointly. Statistics for value are only gathered by the Bureau for owner-occupied condominium units and for specified owner-occupied units (single family houses on less than ten acres, and with no business on the property).

VICTIMIZATION see CRIME.

VIOLENT CRIME see CRIME.

VOTING AGE POPULATION

   All persons over the age of 18 (the voting age for federal elections) in a given geographic area comprise the voting age population. The voting age population does include a small number of persons who, although of voting age, are not eligible to vote (e.g. resident aliens, inmates of institutions, etc.). The voting age population is estimated in even numbered years by the Bureau of the Census.

WAGES AND SALARIES

   Wages and salaries are a type (subgroup) of money income and include civilian wages and salaries, Armed Forces pay and allowances, piece-rate payments, commissions, tips, National Guard or Reserve pay (received for training periods), and cash bonuses before deductions for taxes, pensions, union dues, etc. See also **Money Income.**

WIDOWED PERSONS see **MARITAL STATUS.**

WORK DISABILITY

   A health condition which limits the kind or amount of work a person can do, or prevents working at a job. A person is limited in the kind of work he or she can do if the person has a health condition which restricts his or her choice of jobs. A person is limited in amount of work if he or she is not able to work at a full-time (35 hours or more per week) job or business. See also **Condition (Health).**

WORK-LOSS DAY see **DISABILITY DAY.**

Index